I0868256

THE MAKING OF THE NEW TESTAMENT

By BENJAMIN W. BACON, D.D.

THE MAKING OF THE NEW TESTAMENT

BY

BENJAMIN W. BACON

D.D.

PROFESSOR OF NEW TESTAMENT CRITICISM
AND EXEGESIS IN YALE UNIVERSITY

WIPF & STOCK · Eugene, Oregon

Wipf and Stock Publishers
199 W 8th Ave, Suite 3
Eugene, OR 97401

The Making of the New Testament
By Bacon, Benjamin W.
ISBN 13: 978-1-62032-864-4
Publication date 1/15/2013
Previously published by Williams and Norgate, 1912

CONTENTS

PART I

CANONIZATION AND CRITICISM

PART II

THE LITERATURE OF THE APOSTLE

PART III

THE LITERATURE OF CATECHIST AND PROPHET

PART IV

THE LITERATURE OF THE THEOLOGIAN

THE MAKING OF THE NEW TESTAMENT

PART I

CANONIZATION AND CRITICISM

CHAPTER I

INSPIRATION AND CANONIZATION

THE New Testament presents the paradox of a literature born of protest against the tyranny of a canon, yet ultimately canonized itself through an increasing demand for external authority. This paradox is full of significance. We must examine it more closely.

The work of Jesus was a consistent effort to set religion free from the deadening system of the scribes. He was conscious of a direct, divine authority. The broken lights of former inspiration are lost in the full dawn of God's presence to His soul.

So with Paul. The key to Paul's thought is his revolt against legalism. It had been part of his servitude to persecute the sect which claimed to know another Way besides the "way"[1] of the scribes. These Christians signalized their faith by the rite of baptism, and gloried in the sense of endowment with "the Spirit." Saul was profoundly conscious of the yoke; only he had not dreamed that his own deliverance could come from such a quarter. But contact with victims of the type of Stephen, men "filled with the Spirit," conscious of the very "power from God" for lack of which his soul was fainting, could not but have some effect. It came suddenly, overwhelmingly. The real issue, as Saul saw it, both before and after his conversion, was Law *versus* Grace. In seeking "justification" by favour of Jesus these Christians were opening a new and living way to acceptance with God. Traitorous and apostate as the attempt must seem while the way of the Law still gave promise of success, to souls sinking like Saul's deeper and deeper into the despairing consciousness of "the weakness of the flesh" forgiveness in the name of Jesus might prove to be light and life from God. The despised sect of 'sinners' whom he had been persecuting expressed the essence of their faith in the doctrine that the gift of the Spirit of Jesus had made them sons and heirs of God. If the converted Paul in turn is uplifted—"energized," as he terms it—even beyond his fellow-Christians, by

[1] *Tarik*, i. e. "way," is still the Arabic term for a sect, and the Rabbinic term for legal requirement is *halacha*, i. e. "walk."

the sense of present inspiration, it is no more than we should expect.

Paul's conversion to the new faith—or at least his persistent satisfaction in it—will be inexplicable unless we appreciate the logic of his recognition in it of an inherent opposition to the growing demands of legalism. Jesus had, in truth, led a revolt against mere book-religion. His chief opponents were the scribes, the devotees and exponents of a sacred scripture, the Law. "Law" and "Prophets," the one prescribing the conditions of the expected transcendental Kingdom, the other illustrating their application and guaranteeing their promise, constituted the canon of the synagogue. Judaism had become a religion of written authority. Jesus set over against this a direct relation to the living Father in heaven, ever presently revealed to the filial spirit. The Sermon on the Mount makes the doing of this Father's will something quite other than servitude to written precepts interpreted by official authority and imposed under penalty. It is to be self-discipline in the Father's spirit of disinterested goodness, as revealed in everyday experience.

Even the reward of this self-discipline, the Kingdom, Jesus did not conceive quite as the scribes. To them obedience in this world procured a "share in the world to come." To Him the reward was more a matter of being than of getting. The Kingdom was an heir-apparency; and, therefore, present as well as future. It was "within" and "among" men as well as before them. They should seek to "be sons and daughters of the Highest," taking for granted that all other good things would be "added." So Jesus made religion live again. It became spiritual, inward, personal, actual.

After John the Baptist's ministry to what we should call the 'unchurched' masses, Jesus took up their cause. He became the "friend" and champion of the "little ones," the "publicans and sinners," the mixed 'people of the land' in populous, half-heathen, Galilee. The burdens imposed by the scribes in the name of 'Scripture' were accepted with alacrity by the typical Pharisee unaffected by Pauline misgivings of 'moral inability.' To "fulfil all righteousness" was to the Pharisee untainted by Hellenism a pride and delight. To the "lost sheep of Israel" whom Jesus addressed, remote from temple and synagogue, this "righteousness" had proved (equally as to Paul, though on very different grounds) "a yoke which neither we nor our fathers were able to bear." Jesus "had compassion on the multitude." To them he "spoke with authority"; and yet "not as the scribes" but as "a prophet." When challenged by the scribes for his authority he referred to "the baptism of John," and asked whether John's commission was "from heaven, or of men." They admitted that John was " a prophet." Those who give utterance after this manner to the simple, sincere conviction of the soul, voicing its instinctive aspiration toward " the things that be of God," are conscious that they speak not of themselves.

Jesus, it is true, was no iconoclast. He took pains to make clear that if he superseded what they of old time had taught as righteousness, it was in the interest of a higher, a " righteousness of God." If he disregarded fasts and sabbaths, it was to put substance for form, end for means. " Judgment, mercy, and good faith " should count more than tithes from " mint and anise and cummin." He echoed what John the Baptist had taught of repentance and forgiveness. Hope should no longer be based on birth, or prerogative, or ritual form, but on the mercy of a God who demands that we forgive if we would be forgiven. Such had been, however, the message not of John only, but of all the prophets before him: " I will have mercy, and not sacrifice." Jesus taught this higher, inward, righteousness; but not merely as John had done. John had said: Repent, for the wrath of God is at hand. Jesus said: Repent, for the forgiveness of God is open. The Father's heart yearns over the wayward sons. Jesus preached the nearness of the Kingdom as " glad tidings to the poor "; and among these " poor " were included even aliens who put " faith " in the God of Abraham.

The new Way started from the same Scripture as that of the scribes, but it tended in an opposite direction. Theirs had been gradually developing in definiteness and authority since the time of Ezra; yes, since Josiah had made formal covenant, after the discovery of "the book of the Law" in the temple, pledging himself and his people to obedience. As with many ancient peoples, the codification of the ancient law had been followed by its canonization, and as the national life had waned the religious significance of the Law had increased. It was now declared to express the complete will of God, for an ideal people of God, in a renovated universe, whose centre was to be a new and glorified Jerusalem. The Exile interrupted for a time the process of formal development; but in the ecclesiastical reconstruction which followed in Ezra's time "the book of the Law" had become all the more supreme; the scribe took the place of the civil officer, the synagogue became local sanctuary and court-house in one, the nation became a church, Israel became 'the people of the book.'

Legal requirement calls for the incentive of reward. We need not wonder, then, that the canon of the Law was soon supplemented by that of the writings of the Prophets, historical and hortatory. The former were considered to interpret the Law by showing its application in practice, the latter were valued for their predictive element. Law and Prophets were supplemented by Psalms, and elements from the later literature having application to the religious system. The most influential were the "apocalypses," or "revelations" of the transcendental Kingdom and of the conditions and mode of its coming. Scripture had thus become an embodiment of Israel's religion. It set forth the national law, civil, criminal, or religious; and the national hope, the Kingdom of God. Its custodian and interpreter was the 'scribe,' lawyer and cleric in one. The scribe held "the key of knowledge"; to him it was given to 'bind and loose,' 'open and shut.' Any preacher who presumed to prescribe a righteousness apart from 'the yoke of the Law,' or to promise forgiveness of sins on other authority, must reckon with the scribes. He would be regarded as seeking to 'take the Kingdom by violence.'

Jesus' martyrdom was effected through the priests, the temple authorities; but at the instigation of the scribes and Pharisees. His adherents were soon after driven out from orthodox Judaism and subjected to persecution. This persecution, however, soon found its natural leadership, not among the Sadducean temple-priesthood, but among the devotees of the Law. It was "in the synagogues." From having been quasi-political it became distinctly religious. This persecution by the Pharisees is on the whole less surprising than the fact that so many of the

Jewish believers should have continued to regard themselves as consistent Pharisees, and even been so regarded by their fellow-Jews. In reality Jewish Christians as a rule could see no incompatibility between average synagogue religion and their acceptance of Jesus as the man supernaturally attested in the resurrection as destined to return bringing the glory of the Kingdom. Jesus' idea of 'righteousness' did not seem to them irreconcilable with the legalism of the scribes; still less had they felt the subtle difference between his promise "Ye shall be sons and daughters of the Highest" and the apocalyptic dreams which they shared with their fellow-Jews. Saul the persecutor and Paul the apostle were more logical. In Gal. ii. 15–21 we have Paul's own statement of the essential issue as it still appeared to his clear mind. Average synagogue religion still left room for a more fatherly relation of God to the individual, in spite of the gradual encroachment of the legalistic system of the scribes. Men not sensitive to inconsistency could find room within the synagogue for the 'paternal theism' of Jesus, even if this must more and more be placed under the head of 'uncovenanted mercies.' To Paul, however, the dilemma is absolute. One must trust either to "law" or "grace." Partial reliance on the one is to just that extent negation of faith in the other. The system of written precept permits no exception, tolerates no divided allegiance. If the canon of written law be the God-given condition of the messianic promise, then no man can aspire to share in the hope of Israel who does not submit unreservedly to its yoke. Conversely, faith is not faith if one seek to supplement it by the merit of "works of law."

From this point of view the Jew who seeks forgiveness of sins by baptism "into the name of Jesus" must be considered an apostate from the Law. He acknowledges thereby that he is following another Way, a way of "grace," a short-cut, as it were, to a share in Israel's messianic inheritance by the "favour" of a pretended Messiah. The same Paul who after his conversion maintains (Gal. ii. 21) that to seek "justification" through the Law makes the grace of God of none effect, must conversely have held before conversion that to seek it by "grace" of Jesus made the Law of none effect. Even at the time of writing the axiom still held : No resistance to the yoke of the Law, no persecution (Gal.v. 11).

It is true, then, that the legalistic system of prescription and reward had developed—could develope—only at the expense of the less mechanical, more fatherly, religion of a Hosea or an Isaiah. Even scribes had admitted that the law of love was "much more than all whole burnt-offering and sacrifice." And the movement of the Baptist and of Jesus had really been of the nature of a reaction toward this older, simpler faith.

The sudden revolt in Paul's own mind against the scribal system might not have occurred in the mind of a Pharisee unfamiliar with Greek ideas. But to some extent Paul's experience of the conflict of flesh and spirit, a 'moral inability' to meet the Law's demands *was* a typical Christian experience, as Paul felt it to be. To him it became the basis of an independent gospel. To him the Cross and the Spirit imparted from the risen Messiah were tokens from God that the dispensation of Law is ended and a dispensation of Grace and Sonship begun. Without this Pauline gospel *about* Jesus Christianity could never have become more than a sect of reformed Judaism.

The teaching and martyrdom of Jesus had thus served to bring out a deep and real antithesis. Only, men who had not passed like Paul from the extreme of trust in legalism to a corresponding extremity of despair might be pardoned for some insensibility to this inconsistency. We can appreciate that James and Peter might honestly hold themselves still under obligation of the written law, even while we admit Paul's logic that any man who had once "sought to be justified in Christ" could not turn back in any degree to legal observance without being "self-condemned."

Christianity may be said to have attained self-consciousness as a new religion in the great argument directed by Paul along the lines of his own gospel against Peter and the older apostles. Its victory as a universal religion of 'grace' over the limitations of Judaism was due to the common doctrine of 'the Spirit.' This was the one point of agreement, the one hope of ultimate concord among the contending parties. All were agreed that endowment with 'the Spirit' marks the Christian. It was in truth the great inheritance from Jesus shared by all in common. And Peter and James admitted that to deny that uncircumcized Gentiles had received the Spirit was to "contend against God."

After Paul's death ecclesiastical development took mostly the road of the synagogue. The sense of the presence and authority of 'the Spirit' grew weaker, the authority of the letter stronger. From the outset even the Pauline churches, in ritual, order, observance, had followed instinctively this pattern. All continued, as a matter of course, to use the synagogue's sacred writings. Paul himself, spite of his protest against "the letter," could make no headway against his opponents, save by argument from 'Scripture.' He had found in it anticipations and predictions of his own Christian faith; but by an exegesis often only little less forced and fantastic than that of the rabbinic schools in which he had been trained. This was a necessity of the times. The reasoning, fallacious as it seems to-day, had appealed to and strengthened

Paul's own faith, and was probably effective with others, even if the faith really rested on other grounds than the reasoning by which it was defended. The results of this biblicism were not all salutary. The claims of written authority were loosened rather than broken. Paul himself had found room enough within these defences for the religion of the Spirit; but a generation was coming with less of the sense of present inspiration. Dependence on past authority would be increased in this new generation in direct proportion to its sense of the superior 'inspiration' of the generation which had gone before. Paul is unhampered by even "the scriptures of the prophets" because in his view these take all their authority and meaning from "the Lord, the Spirit." Hence "where the Spirit of the Lord is, there is liberty." Only the remembered "word of the Lord" has authority for Paul beyond his own, even when he thinks that he also has the Spirit. With that exception past revelation is for Paul subordinate to present. But Paul's immediate disciple, the author of Hebrews, is already on a lower plane. This writer looks back to a threefold source of authority: God had spoken in former ages "by the prophets" and to the present "by a Son," but he looks also to an apostolic authority higher than his own: The word "was confirmed unto us by them that heard, God also bearing witness with them, both by signs and wonders, and by manifold powers, and by gifts of the Holy Ghost." Similarly the author of the Pastoral Epistles (90–100 ?) holds the " pattern of sound words " heard from Paul as a " sacred deposit," which is " guarded," rather than revealed, " by the Holy Spirit." The " sound words " in question are defined to be " the words of our Lord Jesus Christ." These, taken together with " the doctrine which is according to godliness," fix the standard of orthodoxy. To " Jude " (100–110 ?) the faith is something " once for all delivered to the saints." His message is : " Remember, beloved, the words spoken before by the apostles of our Lord Jesus Christ." Authority increases, the sense of the revealing Spirit decreases.

It is long before the sense of present inspiration, both in word and work is lost; still longer before the recorded precepts of Jesus, the exhortations and directions of apostles, the visions of " prophets," come to take their place alongside the Bible of the synagogue as " writings of the new covenant." Melito of Sardis (*c.* 170) is the first to use this expression, and even in his case it does not bear the sense of a canon with definite limits. Tertullian (200–210) is the first to place a definite " New Testament " over against the Old. We must glance at some of the intermediate steps to appreciate this gradual process of canonization.

At first there is no other ' Scripture ' than the synagogue's. Clement of Rome (95) still uses only the Law and the Prophets (including certain apocrypha now lost) as his Bible. He refers to the precepts of Jesus (quoted as in Acts xx. 35 from oral tradition), with the same sense as Paul of their paramount authority, and bids the Corinthians whom he addresses give heed to what the blessed Apostle Paul had written to them "in the beginning of the gospel service," to warn them against factiousness. Nor has Clement yet lost the sense of direct inspiration; for he attaches to his own epistle, written in behalf of the church at Rome, the same superhuman authority claimed in Acts xv. 28 for the letter sent by the church at Jerusalem. If the Corinthians disregard the "words spoken by God through us" they will "incur no slight transgression and danger," for these warnings of a sister church are uttered in the name and by inspiration of the Holy Ghost. Still, Clement does not dream of comparing his authority, even when he writes as agent of the church, with that of "the oracles of the teaching of God," the "sacred Scriptures," the "Scriptures which are true, which were given through the Holy Ghost, wherein is written nothing unrighteous or counterfeit." He does not even rank his own authority with that of "the good apostles, Peter and Paul."

Ignatius, bishop of Antioch, transported to Rome for martyrdom in 110–117, employs a brief stay among the churches of Asia to exhort them to resist the encroachments of heresy by consolidation of church organization, discipline, strict obedience to the bishop. Ignatius, too, still feels the afflatus. His message, he declares with emphasis, was revealed to him, together with the occasion for it, directly from heaven. It was "the voice of God and not only of a man" when he cried out among the Philadelphians: "Give heed to the bishop, and the presbytery and deacons." Yet Ignatius cannot enjoin the Romans as Peter and Paul did. They were "apostles." He is "a convict." His inspiration, however undoubted, is of a lower order.

Hermas, a 'prophet' of the same Roman church as Clement, though a generation later, is still so conscious of the superhuman character of his "Visions," "Parables," and "Mandates" that he gives them out for circulation as inspired messages of the Spirit; and this not for Rome alone. Clement, then apparently still living, and "the one to whom this duty is committed," is to send them "to foreign cities." In point of fact the *Shepherd* of Hermas long held a place for many churches as part of the New Testament canon. Yet less than a generation after Hermas, the claim to exercise the gift of prophecy in the church was looked upon as dangerous if not heretical.

In the nature of the case it was really impossible that the original sense of endowment with "the Spirit" should survive. Not only did the rapidly growing reverence for the apostles and the Lord open a chasm separating "the word of wisdom and the word of power" given to that age, from the slighter contemporary claims of miracle and revelation; the very growth and wide dissemination of the gospel message made standardization imperative. Before the middle of the second century Gnostic schism had swept nearly half the church into the vortex of speculative heresy. Marcion at Rome (*c.* 140) carried Pauline anti-legalism to the extreme of an entire rejection of the Old Testament. Judaism and all its works and ways were to be repudiated. The very God of Abraham, Isaac, and Jacob was declared other than, and ignorant of, the "heavenly Father" of Jesus. Against such vagaries there must be some historic standard. Even Marcion himself looked to the past, however recent, as the source of light, and since some written standard must be found, it was he, the heretic, who gave to Christianity its first canon of Christian writings. The Marcionite churches did away with the public reading of the Law and the Prophets, and could only put in their place "Gospel" and "Apostle." Not that Epistles, Gospels, and even 'Revelations' were not also in use among the orthodox; but they are not yet referred to as 'Scripture.' Even gospels are treated merely as aids to the memory in transmitting the teaching of the Lord. This teaching itself is but the authoritative interpretation of Law and Prophets, and is in turn interpreted by the writings of the apostles.

Marcion's 'Gospel' consisted of our Luke, expurgated according to his own ideas. His 'Apostle' contained the Epistles of Paul minus the Pastoral Epistles and a series of passages cancelled out from the rest as Jewish interpolations. This was the first Christian Bible distinct from 'the Scriptures' of the synagogue.

Indirectly the growth of Gnostic heresy contributed still more to the increasing authority of apostolic and quasi-apostolic writings. One of its earliest and most obnoxious forms was called 'Doketism,' from its exaggeration of Paulinism into a complete repudiation of the historic Jesus, whose earthly career was stigmatized as mere 'phantasm' (*dokesis*). Doketism is known to us not only through description by orthodox opponents, but by a few writings of its own. It is the type of heresy antagonized in the Johannine Epistles (*c.* 100) and in those of Ignatius (110–117). Now Ignatius, as we have seen, relied mainly on church organization and discipline. The Pastoral Epistles (90–100), while they emphasize also "the form of healthful words, even the words of our Lord Jesus" take, on the whole, a similar direction. But 1st John, which relies far less than the Pastoral Epistles or Ignatius on mere church organization, is also driven back upon the life and teaching of Jesus as the historic standard. It *does*, therefore, make formal appeal to the sacred tradition in both its elements, but with a difference characteristic of the Pauline spirit. The redeeming life and death of Jesus are viewed as a manifestation of "the life, even the eternal life (of the Logos) which was with the Father and was manifested unto us" (the historic body of believers). Again Jesus' one "new commandment," the law of love, is the epitome of all righteousness.

In his doctrine of Scripture as in many other respects the Johannine writer shows a breadth and catholicity of mind which almost anticipates the development of later ages. His task was in fact the adjustment of the developed Pauline gospel to a type of Christianity more nearly akin to synagogue tradition. This type had grown up under the name of Peter. On the question of the standard of written authority 'John'[1] leaves room for the freedom of the Spirit so splendidly set forth in the teaching and example of Jesus and Paul, while he resists the erratic licence of "those that would lead you astray." The result is a doctrine of historic authority in general, and of that of the Scriptures in particular, sharply differentiated from the Jewish, and deserving in every re-

[1] In using traditional names and titles such as "Luke," "John," "Matthew," "James," no assumption is made as to authenticity. The designation is employed for convenience irrespective of its critical accuracy or inaccuracy.

spect to be treated as the basis of the Christian. In a great chapter of his Gospel (John v.), wherein Jesus debates with the scribes the question of His own authority, the dialogue closes with a denunciation of them because they search the Scriptures with the idea that in them they have eternal life, that is, they treat them as a code of precepts, obedience to which will be thus rewarded. On the contrary, says Jesus, the Scriptures only " bear witness " to the life that is present in Himself as the incarnate, eternal, Word; " but ye will not come unto me that ye might have life."

In seeking the life behind the literature as the real revelation, the Johannine writer makes the essential distinction between Jewish and Christian doctrine. He stands between Paul, whose peculiar view was based on an exceptional personal experience, and the modern investigator, who can but treat all literary monuments and records of religious movements objectively, as data for the history and psychology of religion. If the student be devoutly minded the Scriptures will be to him, too, however conditioned by the idiosyncrasies of temporal environment and individual character, manifestations of " the life, even the eternal life, which was with the Father and was manifested unto us."

But the Johannine writer was far deeper and more 'spiritual'[1] than the trend of

[1] The Fourth Gospel is thus characterized by Clement of Alexandria, meaning that it had a deep symbolic sense.

his age. Ignatius' friend and contemporary, Polycarp, "the father of the Christians" of Asia, in his Epistle to the Philippians (110–117) urges avoidance of the false teachers who "pervert the sayings of the Lord to their own lusts, denying the (bodily) resurrection and judgment." But he has no better remedy than to "turn (probably in a somewhat mechanical way) to the tradition handed down from the beginning" and to study "the Epistles of Paul." The former process is in full application in Polycarp's later colleague, Papias of Hierapolis (*c.* 145 ?), who publishes a little volume entitled *Interpretation of the Sayings of the Lord.* It is based on carefully authenticated traditions of the 'apostles and elders,' especially a certain contemporary "Elder John" who speaks for the Jerusalem succession. According to Papias our two Greek Gospels of Matthew and Mark represent two apostolic sources, the one an Aramaic compilation of the Precepts of Jesus by Matthew, the other anecdotes of his "sayings and doings" collated from the preaching of Peter.

Grateful as we must be for Papias' efforts to authenticate evangelic tradition, since they are corroborated in their main results by all other ancient tradition as well as by critical study of the documents, it is noticeable how they stand in line with the tendencies of the age. Eusebius (325) characterizes the reign of Trajan (98–117) as a period when many undertook to disseminate in writing "the divine Gospels." One of our own evangelists, whose work must probably be referred to the beginning of this period, but is not mentioned by 'the Elder,' alludes to the same phenomenon. The apostles were gone. Hence to Luke [1] the question of "order" was a perplexity, as the Elder observes that it had already been to Mark. Soon after Luke and Papias comes Basilides with his *Exegetics*, probably based on Luke (120 ?), and Marcion (140), both engaged from their own point of view with the current questions of Jesus' teaching and ministry.

Thus, at the beginning of the second century, the elements necessary to the formation of a New Testament canon were all at hand. They included the tradition of the teaching and work of Jesus, the letters of apostles and church leaders revered as given by authority of the Spirit and the visions and revelations of 'prophets.' Not only the elements were present, the irresistible pressure of the times was certain to force them into crystallization. The wonder is not that the canon should have been formed, but that it should have been delayed so long.

For there were also resistant factors. Phrygia, the scene of Paul's first great missionary conquests, the immemorial home of religious enthusiasm, became the seat, about the middle of the second century, of a

[1] See note above, p. 24.

movement of protest against the church policy of consolidation and standardization. Montanus arose to maintain the persistence in the church of the gift of prophecy, tracing the succession in both the male and female line back to Silas the companion of Paul and the prophesying daughters of Philip the Evangelist. The 'Phrygians,' as they were called, naturally made much of the writings current in Asia Minor, especially the book of 'prophecy' attributed to 'John.' Theoretically indeed the church was unwilling to acknowledge the disappearance of this gift. To Hermas (130–140) and the *Teaching of the Twelve* (120–130) it is still a "sin against the Spirit" to interrupt or oppose a prophet during his ecstatic utterance. On the other hand, the *Teaching* reiterates the apostolic warnings to "try the spirits," with prohibitions of specific excesses of the order. Moreover by the time of Montanus and the 'Phrygians' theoretical recognition of revelation through the prophets was rapidly giving way before the practical dangers inseparable from 'revelations' of this enthusiastic character, of which any member of the church, man or woman, ignorant or learned, lay or cleric, might be the recipient. The strict regulative control imposed by both Paul and John[1] upon this type of spiritual gift (1st Thess. v. 20 *f.*; 1st Cor. xii. 3; xv. 29 *f.* 32; *cf.* 1st John iv. 1) was found to be doubly necessary

[1] See note above, p. 24.

in face of the disintegrating tendencies of the post-apostolic age, and after long debate and much protest the movement of Montanus was at last decreed heretical at Rome, though Irenæus (186) interceded for it, and Tertullian (210) became a convert.

The history of this movement in the formative period of the New Testament canon explains why the "revelations of the prophets" obtained but scant recognition as compared with the "word of the Lord" and the "commandment of the apostles." Last of the three, in order of rank (1st Cor. xii. 28; Eph. iv. 11), last also to be codified in written form, we need not be surprised that our present New Testament retains but a single one of the once current books of 'prophecy.' For a time the *Shepherd* of Hermas and the *Apocalypse of Peter* rivalled the claims to canonicity of our own Revelation of John, but were soon dropped. Our own Apocalypse has suffered more opposition than any other New Testament writing, being still excluded from the canon in some branches of the church. Its precarious place at the end of the canon which we moderns have inherited from Athanasius (*ob.* 373) was due, in fact, far less to its author's vigorous assertions of authority as an inspired "prophet" (i. 1–3; xxii. 6–9, 18 *f.*) than to the claims to apostolicity put forward in the preface and appendix. For until the third century no one dreamed of understanding the "John" of Rev. i. 4, 9 and xxii. 8 otherwise than as the Apostle. Eusebius accordingly (325) is uncertain only as to whether the book should be classed in his first group of "accepted" writings, along with the Gospels and Pauline Epistles, or in the third as "spurious." If written by "some other John than the Apostle" he would not even honour it with a place in his second group of "disputed" books, along with Hebrews, James, Jude, and 2nd Peter.

Thus at the end of the second century, while there was still much dispute (destined indeed to continue for centuries) as to the *limits* of the New Testament canon, there had in fact come to be a real canonical New Testament set over against the Old, as of equal, or even greater authority. The "word of the Lord," the "commandment of the apostles," and at last even the "revelations of the prophets," had successively ceased as living realities, and become crystallized into written form. They had been codified and canonized. The church had travelled the beaten track of the synagogue, and all the more rapidly from the example set before it. None of the early canons (*i. e.* lists of writings permitted to be read in the churches) coincides exactly, it is true, with the New Testament current among ourselves. The list of Athanasius is the first to give just our books. The Roman list of the Muratorian fragment (185–200) omits Hebrews, James and 2nd Peter, and gives at least a partial sanction to the *Apocalypse of Peter*.

The lists of Origen (*ob.* 251) and Eusebius (325) vary as respects both inclusion and exclusion. All early authorities express a doubtful judgment regarding the outer fringe of minor writings such as James, Jude, 2nd Peter, 2nd and 3rd John. Even those of larger content, such as Hebrews and Revelation, if their apostolicity was questioned, remained subjects of dispute. But already by A.D. 200 the time had long since passed when any of the thirteen epistles bearing the name of Paul could be deemed open to question. Marcion's exclusion of the three Pastorals had been forgotten. Dispute of the four-gospel canon could still be tolerated; but not for long. Irenæus (186) has no patience with "those wretched men" who cannot see that in the nature of the case there should be neither more nor less than this number. But he explicitly refers to those who disputed "that aspect of the gospel which is called John's." There were, in fact, opponents of Montanism at Rome, who under the lead of Gaius had denied the authenticity of all the writings attributed to John, including the Gospel itself. But even those of the orthodox who were willing enough to reject Revelation, with its now unfashionable eschatology, agreed that Gaius' attack upon the fourth Gospel was too radical. The small body who continued for a few generations to resist the inclusion of any of the Johannine writings in the canon remained without influence, and were ultimately forgotten. The 'catholic'[1] church had repudiated heresy, standardized the faith, and confined its recognized historic expression to a 'canon' of New Testament Scripture.

[1] Catholic is here used in its etymological sense of "general" or universal. We shall have occasion to apply the term in a more limited sense hereafter.

CHAPTER II

THE REACTION TO CRITICISM

THE consolidated 'catholic' church of the third century might seem, so far as its doctrine of Scripture was concerned, to have retraced its steps to a standpoint corresponding completely to that of the synagogue. Only, the paradox still held that the very writings canonized were those supremely adapted to evoke a spirit of resistance to the despotism of either priest or scribe. The Protestant Reformation was a revolt against the former, and it is noticeable how large a part was played by the New Testament doctrine of the 'Spirit' in this struggle of spiritual democracy against hierocratic tyranny. Paul's Epistle to the Galatians became Luther's Palladium.

But the post-Reformation dogmatists took fright at their own freedom. The prediction of the Romanists that repudiation of traditional authority in its ecclesiastical embodiment would result in internecine schism and conflict seemed on the point of being realized. The theological system-makers, like their predecessors of the post-apostolic age, could see no way out but to throw all their weight on a past inspiration assumed to be without error. The canonical books were declared to furnish an infallible rule of faith and practice.

It was in the sincere desire to meet the requirements of this theory that the science of criticism grew up. In the earlier days it did not venture for the most part beyond what is known as 'textual' criticism. For a doctrine of inerrancy is manifestly unserviceable until errors of transmission have been eliminated. Textual criticism set itself to this task, asking the question: As between the various readings found in different New Testament manuscripts, which is original? Unfortunately, to meet the logical requirement the critic, if not backed like those of Rome by a papal guarantee, must himself be infallible. The inevitable result of this attempt, begun in the sincerest spirit of apologetics, was to prove that an infallible text is hopelessly unattainable. Textual criticism is indispensable; but as the servant of apologetics it is foredoomed to failure.

The variation of the manuscripts was not the only obstacle to biblical infallibility. To say nothing of differences of interpretation there was the question of the canon. Either the decision of the 'catholic' church must be accepted as infallible, or scholarship must undertake a 'criticism of the canon' to defend the current list of "inspired" books. A 'higher' criticism became necessary if only to vindicate the church's choice on historical grounds. Roman Catholics like Simon, whose *Critical History* of the Biblical books appeared in 1689–1695, could reopen the question with impunity. Those who based their authority on the infallibility of Scripture alone could not meet the challenge otherwise than as Michælis did in his *Introduction to the Divine Writings of the New Testament* (1750–1780). Michælis undertook a historical inquiry into the circumstances of origin of each of the canonical books, with the object of proving each to be in reality what tradition declared. The twenty-seven commonly accepted were supposed to have been either written by apostles, or at least so superintended and guaranteed by them, as to cover all with the ægis of an infallibility not conceded to the post-apostolic age. Scholarship in the harness of apologetics again found its task impracticable. Michælis himself confessed it " difficult " to prove authenticity in cases like that of the Epistle of Jude. Conceive the task as the scientific vindication of a verdict rendered centuries before on unknown grounds, but now deprived of official authority, and it becomes inevitably hopeless. Can it be expected that doctors will not disagree on the authenticity or pseudonymity of 2nd Peter, who always have disagreed on this and similar questions, and have just admitted failure to agree in the matter of text ?

For half a century criticism seemed lost in the slough of mere controversy over the (assumed) infallible text, and the (assumed) infallible canon. Apologists fought merely on the defensive, endeavouring to prove that men whose fallibility was admitted had nevertheless pronounced an infallible verdict on the most difficult subjects of literary and historical inquiry. Critics had an easy task in showing that the church's theory of inspiration and canonicity was incorrect; but made no progress toward a constructive explanation of the religious, or even the historical, significance of the literature. Real progress was made only when criticism left off the attempt either to establish or disestablish a 'received' text, or an 'authorized' canon, and became simply an instrument in the hand of the historian, as he seeks to trace to their origins the ideas the church enshrined in her literature because she found them effective in her growth.

For the great awakening in which New Testament criticism 'found itself' as a genuine and indispensable branch of the history of religion, we are largely indebted to the eminent church historian, Ferdinand Christian Baur (*ob.* 1860). Baur gathered up the fragmentary results of a generation of mere negation, a war of independence against the tyranny of dogmatic tradition, and sought to place the New Testament writings in their true setting of primitive church history. His particular views have been superseded. Subsequent study has disproved many of his inferences, and brought from friend and foe far-reaching modifications to his general theory. But, consciously or not, Baur, in making criticism the hand-maid of history, was working in the interest of that constructive, Christian, doctrine of inspired Scripture which an ancient and nameless teacher of the church had described as "witness" to the Life, "even the eternal life, which was with the Father," and is in man, and has been manifested in the origin and historical development of our religion.

The Reformation had been a revolt against the despotism of the priest; this was a revolt against the despotism of the scribe.

Baur gave scant—too scant—consideration to early tradition, making his results unduly negative. None of the New Testament books are dated; few besides the Pauline Epistles embody even an author's name; and these few, 1st and 2nd Peter, James, Jude and Revelation, were (1st Peter alone excepted) just those which even the canon-makers had classified as doubtful, or spurious. Not even a Calvin would support the authenticity of 2nd Peter, a Luther had denied the value of James and Revelation. It had been an easy task for 'criticism of the canon' to show that those who determined its content had not been actuated by considerations of pure science. Those books secured admission which were most widely current as ancient and trustworthy, and whose orthodoxy met the standards of the time. Those were disputed, or rejected, which were less widely current, or unorthodox, or could establish no direct relation to an apostle. It was proper for the critic, once his aim had become not apologetic but historical, to drop once for all the question whether the canon-makers' selection—made not for scientific, but for religious purposes—is good, bad or indifferent. The time had come for him to apply the available evidence to his own scientific question: What relation do these several writings bear to the development of Christianity? It remained to be seen whether he could offer constructive evidence more convincing than tradition.

The latest date to which an undated, or disputed, writing can be assigned is that when the marks of its employment by others, or influence upon them, become undeniable. This is termed the 'external' evidence. The earliest date, conversely, is that to which we are brought down by references in the book itself to antecedent and current events, and writings, or by undeniable marks of their influence. This is termed the 'internal' evidence. Counting tradition as part of the external evidence, modern scientific criticism is able to fix within a few decades the origin of all the New Testament writings, without incurring opposition even from the apologist.

No scholar now dreams of adopting any other method of proof, whatever his doctrinal proclivities. The overwhelming majority are agreed that the period covered, from the earliest Pauline Epistles to the latest brief fulminations against Gnostic Doketism and denial of 'resurrection and judgment,' is included in the century from A.D. 50 to 150.

Baur's conception of the course of events in this momentous century has been described as a theory of historical progress by fusion of opposites in a higher unity. The Hegelian scheme of thesis, antithesis and synthesis had in fact some justification in the recognized phenomena of the development of Christianity. It had sprung from Judaism, overcoming the particularism of that still nationalistic faith by the sense of its mission to the world at large. The conflict acknowledged in all the sources and most vividly reflected in the great Epistles of Paul to the Galatians, Corinthians and Romans, a conflict between those who conceived Christianity as a universal religion, and those who looked upon it as only a reformed, spiritualized and perfected Judaism, was the characteristic phenomenon of the first or apostolic age. It was the struggle of the infant faith against its swaddling bands. The critical historian is compelled to estimate all later, anonymous, accounts of this development in the light of the confessedly earlier, and indubitably authentic records, the four great Epistles of

Paul; for these simply reflect the actual conditions, and are not affected by the later disposition to idealize the story. Thesis and antithesis were therefore really in evidence at the beginnings.

Equal unanimity prevailed as to the close of the period in question. In A.D. 150 to 200, Christianity was solidifying into the 'catholic' church, rejecting extremes of doctrine on both sides, formulating its 'rule of faith,' determining its canon, centralizing administrative control. It had thrown off as heretical upon the extreme left Marcion and the Gnostics, who either repudiated the Jewish scriptures altogether, or interpreted them with more than Pauline freedom. On the extreme right it had renounced the unprogressive Ebionites of Palestine, still unreconciled to Paul, and insistent on submission to the Law for Jew and Gentile, as the condition of a 'share in the world to come.' What could be imagined as to the course of events in the intervening century of obscurity? Must it not have witnessed a progressive divergence of the extremes of Paulinists and Judaizers, coincidently with a rapprochement of the moderates from the side of Peter and that of Paul respectively? Baur's outline seemed thus to describe adequately the main course of events. He relied upon internal evidence to determine the dates of the disputed writings and their relation to it. But 'criticism of the canon' in Baur's own, and in the preceding generation, had come to include among the writings of doubtful date and authenticity not only those disputed in antiquity, and the anonymous narrative books, but also 1st Peter and the minor Epistles of Paul. Nothing strictly apostolic was left save the four great Epistles of Paul.

The theory of Baur and the Tübingen school (for so his followers came to be designated) was broadly conceived and ably advocated. In two vital respects it has had permanent influence. (1) Criticism, as already noted, has ceased to be mere debate about text and canon, and concerns itself to-day primarily with the history of Christian ideas as embodied in its primitive literature. Its problem is to relate the New Testament writings, together with all other cognate material, to the history of the developing religion from its earliest traceable form in the greater Pauline Epistles to where it emerges into the full light of day toward the close of the second century. (2) Again, Baur's outline of the process through which the nascent faith attained to full self-consciousness as a world-religion required correction rather than disproof. It was a grievous mistake to identify Peter, James, and John with those whom Paul bitterly denounces as Judaizing "false brethren," "superextra apostles," "ministers of Satan." It was a perversion of internal evidence to reject as post-Pauline the Epistles of the later period such as Philippians and Colossians, on the ground that Paul himself did not live to participate in the second crisis, the defence of his doctrine against perversion on the side of mystical, Hellenistic theosophy. The great Epistles written under the name of Paul from the period of his captivity are innocent of reference to the developed Gnostic systems of the second century. They antagonize only an incipient tendency in this direction.

But while the transition of A.D. 50–150 was both deeper and more complex than Baur conceived, the transfer of the gospel during that century from Jewish to Gentile soil is really the great outstanding fact, against which as a background the literature must be read; and the initial stage of the process is marked by the controversy of Paul with the Galilean apostles. What we must call, in distinction from Paulinism, 'apostolic' Christianity is well represented in the Book of Acts. Paul's writings show that he felt himself and his churches to represent an independent type of Christianity in all respects equal to the 'apostolic,' the problem being unification of the two. Now it is axiomatic that the investigator must proceed from the relatively known and determinable to the unknown and disputable. Accordingly it is in reality from the Epistolary literature of the church, in particular the greater Pauline Epistles, that he must take his start. As a source for our understanding of the development of the life of the church the Literature of the Apostle, directly participant in the conflicts and issues of the times, even if in its later elements of doubtful or pseudonymous authorship, takes precedence as a whole over the Literature of the Catechist, with its later and more or less idealized narration, exemplified in the Book of Acts.

Modern criticism acknowledges, then, its indebtedness to the Tübingen school for a clearer definition of both its task and method, by concentrating attention upon the contrast between the Petrine and the Pauline conception of 'the gospel.' Still it must be admitted that most of the inferences first drawn have since been overthrown. In their chronological scheme of the New Testament writings the Tübingen critics underestimated the force of the external evidences (including early tradition) and misinterpreted the internal. New discovery and more careful study of literary relations have inverted Baur's views as to dates of the Johannine writings. Four of these (the Gospel and three Epistles) are anonymous. Baur's date for these has been forced back by no less than half a century. The fifth (Revelation) bears the name of John, but was hotly disputed as pseudonymous in the second century, and even by its supporters was dated so late as "the end of the reign of Domitian" (95).

The Tübingen school placed Revelation thirty years earlier, and attributed it to the Apostle. Modern criticism emphatically reverts to the ancient date, and regards the book as pseudonymous, or as written by " some other John."

Again the relative dates of the Synoptic writings (Matthew, Mark, Luke–Acts) were inverted by the Tübingen critics, primarily through wrong application of their theory of doctrinal development; secondarily, and as a consequence, through misinterpretation of the intricate literary relationships. Present-day criticism considers it established that Mark is the oldest of the three, taken up by each of the other two. There is almost equal unanimity in regarding the discourse material common to Matthew and Luke and variously combined by each with Mark, as independently drawn by them from the book of the " Precepts of the Lord," reported by Papias to have been compiled by Matthew " in the Hebrew (*i. e.* Aramaic) tongue." Tübingen gospel criticism is thus almost entirely set aside, in favour of the so-called ' Two-document ' theory.

So with the Pauline Epistles of the second period. Doubt still clings to Ephesians. It had been treated by some as pseudo-Pauline even before the time of Baur; but Baur's own followers soon receded from his extreme application of his theory to the internal evidence of Philippians, Colossians and Philemon. It became evident that Paul's " gospel" included something more than the mere antithesis of Law and Grace. He had other opponents than the Judaizers, and had to defend his doctrine against perversion by Grecizing mystics as well as against opposition by Pharisaic legalists.

Two generations of research and controversy have greatly advanced the cause of constructive criticism. Hand in hand with a more accurate dating of the literature, secured through more impartial judgment of both the external and internal evidence, there has gone a reconstruction of our conception of the course of events. The tendencies in the early church were not two only, but four; corresponding, perhaps, to those rebuked by Paul at Corinth, which called themselves by the names respectively of Peter, of Paul, of Apollos and of Christ. It seems probable from the bitterness with which in 2nd Cor. x. 7 Paul denounces the man who says, "I am of Christ," that this party-cry was employed in the sense of following the example of Jesus as respects obedience to the Law (for even Paul acknowledged that Christ had been "made a minister of the circumcision for the truth of God"). If so, the Corinthian "Christ-party" may be identified with those "ministers of the circumcision" who denied both the apostleship and the gospel of Paul. At all events those "of Cephas" were relatively harmless. They may be identified with the so-called 'weak' of Romans, for whose scruples on the score of 'pollutions of idols' Paul demands such consideration both at Corinth and at Rome. His own adherents both at Corinth (those 'of Paul') and at Rome (the 'strong') are to follow his example not merely in recognizing that: "No idol is anything in the world," that "there is nothing unclean of itself," and that "all things are lawful." It is to be followed also in recognizing the limitations of this liberty. Limits are imposed among other things by the scruples of others, so that Paul himself becomes "as under the Law" when among Jews, though "as without the Law" among the Gentiles. The "weak" are to be resisted only when the admission of themselves or their claims would lead to "doubtful disputations," or to a rebuilding of walls of separation that had been torn down through faith in Christ. Galatians sounds the battle-cry of endangered liberty. Corinthians (and Romans in still higher degree) shows the magnanimity of the victor.

Whether it be possible to identify those "of Apollos" at Corinth with the beginnings of that Hellenistic perversion of the Pauline gospel into a mystical theosophy which afterwards passed into Gnosticism may be left an open question. At least we have come to see that the conditions of the church's growth were far more complex than Baur imagined. In particular it is necessary to distinguish four different attitudes on the single question of the obligation of the Law. There were (1) Judaizers who insisted on complete submission to the Law as the condition of salvation, for both Jews and Gentiles; (2) imitators of Cephas, who considered believers of Jewish birth to be "under the Law," but asked of Gentiles only such consideration for it as the special conditions seemed to require; (3) Paulinists, who held that neither Jews nor Gentiles are under the law, yet felt that consideration should be shown for the scrupulous when asked not as of right, but as of charity; (4) radicals, who recognized no limits to their freedom save the one new commandment.

But while conflict first broke out over the mere concrete question of Gentile liberty, the real distinction of Paul's gospel from that of the older apostles was far deeper. The question as Tübingen critics conceived it concerned primarily the *extent* of the gospel message,—to how large a circle was it offered? Modern criticism has come to see that the difference was in higher degree a difference of *quality*. Paul's whole message of redemption through the cross and resurrection started from other premisses than those of the Galilean apostles, and was conceived in other terms. For this reason it leads over to a new Christology. In short, the transition of Christianity from its Jewish to its Gentile form is not a mere enlargement of its field by the abolition of particularistic barriers. The background we must study for the understanding of it is not so much mere contemporary history as the contemporary history *of religion.* The development from the Petrine gospel broadly characteristic of the Synoptic writings, through the Pauline Epistles to that of the Johannine writings, is a transition from Hebrew to Hellenistic conceptions of what redemption is, and how it is effected. Modern criticism expresses the contrast in its distinction of the gospel *of* Jesus from the gospel *about* Jesus.

In the case of both Paul and his predecessors in the faith there is a common starting-point. It was the doctrine that God had raised Jesus from the dead and exalted Him as Christ and Lord to the throne of glory. Its proofs were the ecstatic phenomena of the Spirit, those strange manifestations of 'prophecy,' 'tongues,' and the like in the Christian assembly. The inference from this resurrection faith for an apostle of the Galilean group was that he must "teach all men everywhere to observe all things whatsoever Jesus had commanded." Jesus had been raised up in Israel as the Prophet like unto Moses; His apostle must repeat the remembered word of commandment and the word of promise. He will have an authority derived from the manifestations of signs and wonders. These had accompanied Jesus' own career, and now, by grace of His endowment of His disciples with the Spirit, they will be repeated by their hands. The 'apostolic' gospel is thus primarily historical. The Pauline gospel centres at the other pole of religious conviction. It is primarily psychological. For Paul the immediate effect of the revelation of God's Son "in" him is an irresistible impulse to relate his own soul's experience. The gospel he preaches is not so much what Jesus did or said while on earth, as what God has done, and is still doing, through the "life-giving Spirit" which emanates from the risen Lord. Signs and wonders are tokens of the Spirit, but are of less value, and must vanish before the "abiding" ethical gifts. Both the Pauline and the Petrine gospel start from the common confession of "Jesus as Lord"; but the Christology of the Synoptic literature is an Apotheosis doctrine, falling back on the historical Jesus. That of the Epistles is a doctrine of Incarnation, appealing to the eternal manifestation of God in man. For the former, Jesus was "a prophet mighty in deed and word," raised up by God in accordance with the promise of Deut. xviii. 18, to turn Israel to repentance. Having fulfilled this mission in rejection and martyrdom Jesus had been exalted to God's "right hand" and "made both Lord and Christ." He there awaits the subjection of all His enemies. In the Pauline gospel the story of Jesus is a drama of the supernal regions, wherein His earthly career as prophet, leader, teacher, sinks to the level of the merest episode. As pre-existent spirit, Jesus had been from the beginning of the creation "in the form of God." As the period of its consummation drew near He took upon Him human form, descended through suffering and death to the lowest depths of the underworld, and by divine power had reascended above all the heavens with their ranks of angelic hierarchies. Whether Paul himself so conceived it or not, the Gentile world had no other moulds of thought wherein to formulate such a Christology than the current myths of Redeemer-gods. The value of the individual *soul* had at last been discovered, and men resorted to the ancient personifications of the forces of nature as deliverers of this new-found *soul* from its weakness and mortality. The influential religions of the time were those of personal redemption by mystic union with a dying and resurrected "Saviour-god," an Osiris, an Adonis, an Attis, a Mithra. Religions of this type were everywhere displacing the old national faiths. The Gentile could not think of "the Christ" primarily as a Son of David who restores the kingdom to Israel, shatters the Gentiles like a potter's vessel and rules them with a rod of iron. If he employed this Old Testament language at all, it had for him a purely symbolical sense. The whole conception was spiritualized. The "enemies" overcome were the spiritual foes of humanity, sin and death; "redemption" was not the deliverance of Israel out of the hand of all their enemies, that (together with all afar off that call upon the name of this merciful God) they may "serve Him in holiness and righteousness all their days." It was the rescue of the sons of Adam out of the bondage to evil Powers incurred through inheritance of Adam's sinful flesh. This had been the tendency already of Jewish apocalypse. The starting-point of Paul's own conceptions was not Israel's bondage in Egypt, but a conception already tinged, like the late book of Jewish philosophy called the Wisdom of Solomon, with the Stoic conception of 'flesh' as prison-house of 'spirit,' already inflamed, like the contemporary Jewish apocalypses of Esdras and Baruch, with lurid visions of a universe rescued by superhuman power from a thraldom of demonic rule. Paul's preaching was made real by his own experience. For if ever there was an evangelist whose message was his own experience, Paul was such. And Paul's experience was not so much that of a Palestinian Jew, as that of a Hellenist, one whose whole idea of 'redemption' has been unconsciously universalized, individualized, and spiritualized, by contact with Greek and Hellenistic thought. Paul and the Galilean apostles were not far apart in their expectations of the future. Both stood gazing up into heaven. But for his authority Paul inevitably looked inwards, the Galilean apostles looked backwards.

It is hopeless at the present stage of acquaintance with the history of religion, particularly the spread of the various 'mysteries' and religions of personal redemption in the early empire, to deny this contrast between the gospel of Paul and the gospel of "the apostles and elders at Jerusalem." It is shortsighted to overlook its significance in the transition of the faith. Whereas the Jewish-Christian had as its principal background the national history, more or less transcendentalized in the forms of apocalypse, Paul's had as its principal background the speculative mythology of the Hellenistic world, more or less adapted to the forms of Judaism. Only ignorance of the function of mythology, especially as then employed to express the aspiration of the soul for purity, life and fellowship with God, can make these mythologically framed religious ideas seem an inappropriate vehicle to convey Paul's sense of the significance of Jesus' message and life of "sonship." They were at least the best expression those times and that environment could afford of the greater Kingdom God had proclaimed in the resurrection of the Christ, and was bringing to pass through the outpouring of His Spirit.

Modern criticism must therefore recognize that the beginnings of our religion were not a mere enlargement of Judaism by abolition of the barriers of the Law, but a fusion of the two great streams of religious thought distinctive of the Jewish and the Hellenistic world in a higher unity. Alexander's hoped-for "marriage of Europe and Asia" was consummated at last in the field of religion itself. Denationalized Judaism contributed the social ideal: the messianic hope of a world-wide Kingdom of God. It is the worthy contribution of a highly ethical national religion. Hellenism contributed the individual ideal: personal redemption in mystic union with the life of God. It is a concept derived from the Greek's newly-awakened consciousness of a personality agonizing for deliverance out of the bondage of the material and transitory, alien and degrading to its proper life. The critic who has become a historian of ideas will find his study of the literature of the apostolic and post-apostolic age here widening out into a prospect of unsuspected largeness and significance. He will see as the two great divisions of his subject, (1) the gospel *of* Jesus, represented, as we are told, in the first beginnings of literary development by an Aramaic compilation of the Precepts of the Lord by the Apostle Matthew, circulating possibly even before the great Pauline Epistles among the Palestinian churches; (2) the gospel *about* Jesus, represented in the Pauline Epistles, and these based on their author's personal experience. It is a gospel of God's action "in Christ, reconciling the world." It interprets the personality of Jesus and his experience of the cross and resurrection as manifestations of the divine idea. The interpretation employs Hellenistically coloured forms of thought, and is forced to vindicate itself first against subjection to legalism, afterwards against perversion into an unethical, superstitious theosophy. But surely the doctrine *about* Jesus, interpreting the significance of His person and work as the culmination of redemption through the indwelling of God in men and among men belongs as much to the essence of Christianity as the gospel of love and faith proclaimed *by* Jesus.

Besides these two principal types of gospel and their subordinate combinations the critical historian may see ultimately emerging a type of 'spiritual' gospel, growing upon Gentile soil, in fact, receiving its first literary expression in the early years of the second century at the very headquarters of the Pauline mission-field. This third type aims to be comprehensive of the other two. It is essentially a gospel about Jesus, though it takes the form for its main literary expression of a gospel preached by Jesus. The fourth evangelist is the true successor of Paul, though the conditions of the age compel him to go beyond the literary form of the Epistle and to construct a Gospel wherein both factors of the sacred tradition shall appear, the words and works, the Precepts and the Saving Ministry of Jesus. But it is in no mechanical or slavish sense that the fourth evangelist appeals to this supreme authority. He lifts the whole message above the level of mere baptized legalism, even while he guards it against the unbridled licence of Gnostic theosophy, applying to this purpose his doctrine of the Incarnate Logos. His basis is psychology as well as history. It is the Life which is the light of men, that life whose source is God, and which permeates and redeems His creation; even "the eternal Life which was with the Father and was manifested to us."

In the critical grouping of our New Testament writings the Gospel and Epistles of John can occupy, then, no lesser place than that of the keystone of the arch.

To sum up: the Literature of the Apostle owed its early development and long continuance among the Pauline churches of Asia Minor and Greece, to the impetus and example of Paul's apostolic authority. The Literature of the Teacher and Prophet, growing up around Jerusalem and its daughter churches at Antioch and Rome, came slowly to surpass in influence the "commandment of the apostles," as the church became more and more exclusively dependent upon it for the "teaching of the Lord." It was the function of the great "theologian" of Ephesus (as he came early to be called), linking the authority of both, to furnish the fundamental basis for the catholic faith.

PART II

THE LITERATURE OF THE APOSTLE

CHAPTER III

PAUL AS MISSIONARY AND DEFENDER OF THE GOSPEL OF GRACE

MOST vital of all passages for historical appreciation of the great period of Paul's missionary activity and its literature is the retrospect over his career as apostle to the Gentiles and defender of a gospel "without the yoke of the Law" in Gal. i.–ii. Especially must the contrast be observed between this and the very different account in Acts ix.–xvi.

Galatians aims to counteract the encroachments of certain Judaizing interlopers upon Paul's field, and seems to have been written from Corinth, shortly after his arrival there (*c.* 50) on the Second Missionary Journey (Acts xv. 36—xviii. 22). We take "the churches of Galatia" to be those founded by Paul in company with Barnabas on the First Missionary Journey (Acts xiii.–xiv.), and revisited with Silas after a division of the recently evangelized territory whereby Cyprus had been left to Barnabas and Mark (Acts xv. 36—xvi. 5; *cf*. Gal. iv. 13).

The retrospect is in two parts: (1) a proof of the divine origin of Paul's apostleship and gospel by the independence of his conversion and missionary career; (2) an account of his defence of his "gospel of uncircumcision" on the two occasions when it had been threatened. Visiting Jerusalem for the second time some fifteen years[1] after his conversion, he secured from its "pillars," James, Peter, and John, an unqualified, though "private," endorsement. At Antioch subsequently he overcame renewed opposition by public exposure of the inconsistency of Peter, who had been won over by the reactionaries.

Acts reverses Paul's point of view, making his career in the period of unobstructed evangelization one of labour for Jews alone, in complete dependence on the Twelve. It practically excludes the period of opposition by a determination of the Gentile status in an 'Apostolic Council.' Paul is represented as simply acquiescing in this decision.

As described by Paul, the whole earlier period of fifteen years had been occupied by missionary effort for *Gentiles*, first at Damascus, afterwards "in the regions of Syria and Cilicia." It was interrupted only by a

[1] Or perhaps thirteen. Gal. ii. 1 may reckon from the conversion (31–33). In both periods (Gal. i. 18, and ii. 1) both termini are counted.

journey "to Arabia," and later, three years after his conversion, by a two-weeks' private visit to Peter in Jerusalem. In this period must fall most of the journeys and adventures of 2nd Cor. xi. 23–33. It was practically without contact with Judæa. His "gospel" was what God alone had taught him through an inward manifestation of the risen Jesus.

As described by Luke[1] the whole period was spent in the evangelization of Greek-speaking *Jews,* principally at Jerusalem. This was Paul's chosen field, worked under direction of "the apostles." Only against his will[2] was he driven for refuge to Tarsus, whence Barnabas, who had first introduced him to the apostles, brought him to Antioch. There was no Gentile mission until Barnabas and he were by that church made its 'apostles.' This mission was on express direction of "the Spirit" (Acts ix. 19–30; xi. 25 *f.*; xiii. 1–3; *cf.* xxii. 10–21). Paul's apostleship to the Gentiles begins, then, according to Luke, with the First Missionary Journey, when in company with (and at first in subordination to) Barnabas he evangelizes Cyprus and southern Galatia. The two are agents of Antioch, with "letters of commendation" from "the apostles and elders in Jerusalem" (Acts xv. 23–26). Paul is not

[1] We apply the name to the writer of Luke-Acts without prejudice to the question of authorship.

[2] Acts xxii. 10–21 is not quite consistent with xxvi. 15 18; but the general sense is clear.

an apostle of Christ in the same sense as the Twelve (*cf.* Acts i. 21 *f.*). He is a providential "vessel of the Spirit," ordained "by men and through men." His gospel is Peter's unaltered (*cf.* Acts xxvi. 16–23).

There is even wider disparity regarding the period of opposition. Luke slightly postpones its beginning and very greatly antedates its suppression. Moreover, he makes Paul accept a solution which his letters emphatically repudiate.

According to Acts there was no opposition before the First Missionary Journey, for the excellent reason that there had been no Gentile propaganda.[1] There was no opposition after the Council called to consider it (Acts xv.), for the conclusive reason that "the apostles and elders" left nothing to dispute about. As soon as the objections were raised the church in Antioch laid the question before these authorities, sending Paul and Barnabas to testify. On their witness to the grace of God among the Gentiles, Peter (explicitly claiming for himself (!) this special apostleship, Acts xv. 7) proposes unconditional acknowledgment of Gentile liberty, referring

[1] Cornelius' case (Acts x. 1—xi. 18) is exceptional, and no propaganda follows. The reading "Greeks" in Acts xi. 20, though required by the sense and therefore adopted by the English translators, is not supported by the textual evidence. Luke has here corrected his source to suit his theory, just as in x. 1—xi. 18 he passes by the true significance of the story, which really deals with the question of *eating* with Gentiles (xi. 3, 7 *f.*).

to the precedent of Cornelius. In this there was general acquiescence. In fact the matter had really been decided before (Acts xi. 1–18). The only wholly new point was that raised by James in behalf of "the Jews among the Gentiles" (Acts xv. 21; *cf.* xxi. 21). For their sake it is held "necessary" to limit Gentile freedom on four points. They must abstain from three prohibited meats, and from fornication, for these convey the "pollution of idols." The "necessity" lies in the fact that *liberty from the Law is not conceded to Jews.* They will be (involuntarily) defiled if they eat with their Gentile brethren unprotected. "Fornication" is added because (in the words of an ancient Jewish Christian) it "differs from all other sins in that it defiles not only the sinner, but those also *who eat or associate with him.*" Paul and Barnabas, according to Luke, gladly accepted these "decrees," and Paul distributed them "for to keep" among his converts in Galatia (!). *Peter* is the apostle to the Gentiles. Antioch and Jerusalem decide the question of their status. The terms of fellowship are those of *James* and Peter.

Paul has no mention of either Council or 'decrees.' His terms of fellowship positively exclude both. He falls back upon the private Conference, and lays bare a story of agonizing struggle to make effective its recognition of the equality and independence of Gentile Christianity. The struggle is a result of his resistance to emissaries "from James" at Antioch, who had brought over all the Jewish element in that mixed church, including Peter and "even Barnabas" to terms of fellowship acceptable to the Pillars. After the collision at Antioch Paul leaves the "regions of Syria and Cilicia," and transfers the scene of his missionary efforts to the Greek world between the Taurus range and the Adriatic. For the next ten years we see him on the one side conducting an independent mission, proclaiming the doctrine of the Cross as inaugurating a new era, wherein law has been done away, and Jew and Gentile have "access in one Spirit unto the Father." On the other he is defending this gospel of 'grace' against unscrupulous Jewish-Christian traducers, and labouring to reconcile differences between his own followers and those of 'the circumcision' who are not actively hostile, but only have taken 'offence.' Throughout the period, until the arrest in Jerusalem which ends his career as an evangelist, Paul stands alone as champion of unrestricted Gentile liberty and equality. He cannot admit terms of fellowship which imply a continuance of the legal dispensation. Jewish Christians may keep circumcision and the customs if they wish; but may not hold or recommend them as conferring the slightest advantage in God's sight. He will not admit the doctrine of salvation by faith *with* works of law. Jew as well as Gentile must have "died to the Law."

There is no "justification" except "by faith *apart* from works of law."[1]

Unless we distinctly apprehend the deep difference, almost casually brought out by this question of the (converted) Jew among Gentiles and his obligation to eat with his Gentile brother, a difference between 'apostolic' Christianity as Luke gives it, and the 'gospel' of Paul, we can have no adequate appreciation of the great Epistles produced during this period of conflict. The basis of Luke's pleasing picture of peace and concord is a fundamentally different conception of the relation of Law and Grace. Paul and Luke both hold that the Mosaic commandments are not binding on *Gentiles*. The point of difference—and Paul's own account of his Conference with the Pillars goes to show that Luke's idea is also theirs; else why need there be a division of 'spheres of influence'?—is Paul's doctrine that the believing Jew *as well as the Gentile* is "dead to the Law." And this doctrine was never accepted south of the Taurus range.

Agreement and union were sure to come, if only by the rapid disappearance from the church after 70 A.D. of the element of the circumcised, and the progressive realization in 'Syria and

[1] The assertion has recently been made in very high quarters on the basis of 1st Cor. vii. 18 that Paul also took the "apostolic" view that the Christian of Jewish birth remains under obligation to keep the law. One would think Paul had not added verse 19!

Cilicia' of the impracticability of the Jerusalem-Antioch plan of requiring Gentiles to make their tables innocuous to the legalist. If only the participation of Paul and Barnabas be excluded from the story of Acts xv. (or better, restored to its proper sequence after Acts xi. 30) we have every reason to accept Luke's account of an Apostolic Council held at Jerusalem not long after "Peter came to Antioch" to settle between the churches of northern and southern Syria the knotty question of the Christian Jew's eating or not eating with Gentiles. It is almost certain that Syria did adopt this modus vivendi for "the brethren which are of the Gentiles *in Antioch, Syria and Cilicia*" (Acts xv. 23); for we can trace its gradual obsolescence there. In Revelation (a book of Palestinian origin republished at Ephesus *c.* 95; *cf.* Rev. ii. 14, 20, 24) in the *Teaching of the Twelve* (125), and in the 'Western' text of Acts xv. (150 ?) there is a progressive scaling down of the 'burden.' Gentiles are at last asked to do almost nothing more than Paul had demanded on moral grounds without recognition of the validity of "distinctions of meats." In A.D. 120 the 'burden' is: "Concerning meats, keep what thou art able; however, abstain at all events from things offered to idols, for it is the food of dead gods."

But to take Luke's account of how peace was restored, with its implication that the Pauline gospel as developed in Greek Christendom between the Taurus range and the Adriatic was nothing more than a branch from the parent stock of the 'apostolic' church in "Syria and Cilicia," would be like viewing the history of the United States from the standpoint of a British imperialist of a period of Anglo-Saxon reunion in A.D. 2000, who should omit entirely the American War of Independence, holding that Washington and Franklin after bearing testimony before Parliament accepted for the colonies a plan of settlement prepared by a Liberal Government which reduced to a minimum the obnoxious requirements of the Tories.

The history of this period of the development of the independent 'gospel' of Paul and of his independent churches is so vital, and so confused by generations of well-meaning 'harmonizers,' that we must take time to contrast once more Luke's theory of the process of reunion with Paul's.

In Acts Paul takes precisely the view of Peter and James. He is himself 'under the Law.' He does *not* disregard it even among Gentiles. On the contrary, he sets an example of scrupulous legality to the Jews among the Gentiles, himself 'walking orderly, keeping the Law.' The statement that he "teaches them to forsake Moses, telling them not to circumcise their children, nor to obey the customs" is a calumny (!) which he takes public occasion to disprove (Acts xxi. 20–26) Before the Sanhedrin he emphatically declares himself a consistent Pharisee (Acts xxiii. 1, 6); before Felix and Festus, blameless by the standard of Law and Prophets (xxiv. 14–16; xxv. 8); before Agrippa, a strict Pharisee in his conduct hitherto (xxvi. 5, 22 *f*.). Titus, whose circumcision Paul strenuously resisted, is never mentioned in Acts. Conversely Timothy (a Jew only on his mother's side) Paul " took and circumcised " immediately after the Jerusalem Council " because of the Jews that were in those parts " (Galatia !). His visit with Barnabas to Jerusalem is not occasioned by opposition to Gentile missions, though it falls between Barnabas' mission from Jerusalem to investigate the alarming reports of Gentile conversions at Antioch, and the First Missionary Journey on which the two take with them Mark, who had accompanied them from Jerusalem. No; according to Luke Gentile missions did not yet exist [1] (!). This visit (that of the Conference, Gal. ii. 1–10) was merely to convey a gift from the Antioch church to that of Jerusalem because of the famine " about that time " (it occurred in 46–47). Conversely the great ' offering of the Gentiles ' made at the risk of Paul's life in company with delegates from each province of his field, as a proffer of peace, the enterprise which occupies so large a place in his effort and his letters of this period (1st Cor. xvi. 1–6; 2nd Cor. 8–9; Rom. xv. 15, 16, 25–32), has in

[1] On the reading "Greeks" in Acts xi. 20 see note above, p. 59.

Acts no relation to the controversy—for the demonstration of Paul's exemplary legalism in the temple is merely incidental. The gift Paul brought was " alms to my nation " (!) (Acts xxiv. 17). The reader asks in vain what necessitates this dangerous journey. The only motives assigned are a Nazarite vow assumed in Cenchreæ (xviii. 18; xxi. 24), and regard for the Jewish feasts (xx. 16).

The background of history against which the modern reader must place the great letters of Paul of the first period, is manifestly something quite different from the mere unsifted story of Acts. Their real origin is in a profound difference in Paul's idea of 'the gospel' and the necessity of defending the independence of it and of the Gentile churches founded on it. The difference originates in Paul's own religious experience. It found its first expression in his antithesis of Law and Grace, his doctrine that the cross marks the abolition of the economy of Law.

Both in Galatians and everywhere else Paul treats on equal terms with the representatives of the " apostleship of the circumcision." He denounces Peter and " the rest of the Jews," including " even Barnabas," at Antioch, after they have withdrawn from Gentile fellowship in order to preserve their legal 'cleanness,' and the point of the denunciation is that this is inconsistent with *their* (implied) abandonment of the Law as a means of salvation when they " sought to be justified by faith in

Christ." This makes their conduct not only inconsistent but cowardly and "hypocritical."

Here is something far deeper than a mere question of policy. Paul's attitude shows that from the beginning he has really been preaching "a different gospel." A gospel *about* Christ in which the central fact is the cross as the token of the abolition of a dispensation of Law wherein Jew and Gentile alike were in a servile relation to God, under angelic (or demonic) "stewards and governors," and the inauguration of a dispensation of Grace, wherein all who have 'faith' and receive in baptism the gift of 'the Spirit,' are thereby adopted to be God's sons. Beside this cosmic drama of the cross and resurrection wherein God reveals his redemptive purpose for the world, the mere inculcation of the easy yoke of Jesus as a new Law, simplifying and supplementing the old by restoring the doctrine of forgiveness for the repentant believer (*cf.* Matt. xxviii. 20; Acts x. 42 *f.*; xiii. 39; xxvi. 22 *f.*) seems only half a gospel.

Paul can never surrender the independence of his God-given message, nor the liberty wherewith Christ has made all believers free in abolishing the economy of law and making them "sons" by the Spirit. And yet he is even more determined to achieve peace and reunion than the apostles 'of the circumcision'; only he has a different plan. Paul and his churches fall back upon the Jerusalem Conference, not upon the 'Apostolic Council.'

The Conference is their Magna Charta. Its recognition of Paul's independent gospel and apostleship as no less divine than Peter's is their guarantee of liberty and equality; its request for brotherly aid is their promise of fraternity.

Approaches were made on both sides. It is true the ill-advised attempt of the Judaizers to secure unity by a renewal of their propaganda of the Law, seducing the Greek churches from their loyalty to Paul and his gospel, provoked from him only such thunderbolts as Galatians, with its defence of "the liberty wherewith Christ hath made us free," or 2nd Cor. x. 1 to xiii. 10, with its denunciation of the "ministers of Satan." Peace through surrender was not to Paul's mind. But the sincere attempt of the followers of Peter to find a *modus vivendi*, even if they did not venture to claim liberty from the Law for themselves, found Paul prepared to go more than half-way. His epistles are not more remarkable for their strenuous defence of the liberty of sonship, than for their insistence on the obligation of brotherly love. His churches must be not only morally pure for their own sakes, but must avoid offences to the more scrupulous. Even that which Christian liberty allows must be sacrificed to the scruples of the 'weak,' if only it be not "unto doubtful disputations," or demanded as of right. From 1st Thessalonians (Corinth, A.D. 50), where, in the absence of all Judaizing opposition Paul merely exhibits his simple gospel of the resurrection and judgment to come, unaffected by questions of Law and Grace, on through Galatians with its sublime polemic for the liberty of sons, to the Corinthian correspondence, with its insistence on the duty of consideration and forbearance, its stronger note of love, its revelation of the widespread, strenuous exertions of Paul to promote his great 'offering,' down to Romans, where the 'offering of the Gentiles' is ready to be made (Rom. xv. 16–33), and Paul is sedulously preparing to enter a great new field already partially occupied, by presenting a full and superlatively conciliatory statement of his entire 'gospel' (i. 15–17), there is steady progress toward the "peace" and "acceptance" which he hopes to find in Jerusalem. The later Epistles, with their different phase of conflict, the very attitude of 'apostolic' Christianity toward Paul, as exhibited in Acts, make it incredible that substantial unity was not in fact secured.[1] We cannot, indeed, accept Luke's representation of Paul as performing the Nazarite ceremonial in the temple in order to prove *that he does not teach that the Law is not binding on Jews.* But

[1] The actual outcome is seen in the reduction of the 'burden' to the two items of abstinence from "fornication and from things offered to idols." Paul's nicer distinctions under the latter head (1st Cor. viii. 1–13, x. 14–23) as well as his distinction between the ceremonial and the moral grounds for abstinence, were disregarded.

it does not follow that Paul may not have done even this to prove that his principle of accommodation to the weak (1st Cor. ix. 19–22) left ample room for fellowship with the Jewish Christian—except when (as with Peter and Barnabas at Antioch) the needless scruples of the legalist were made a pretext for "compelling the Gentiles to live as do the Jews."

Had unity been attained through the simple process imagined by Luke, obedient acquiescence of Paul and the Gentiles in the divinely inspired verdict of "the apostles and elders in Jerusalem," Christianity would have been an immeasurably poorer thing than it became. Indeed, it is questionable whether a gospel of mere simplification, extension and supplementation of the Law would ever have made permanent conquest of the Gentile world. It is because Paul stood out on this question of 'meats' for the equal right of his independent gospel, refusing submission until his great ten-years' work of evangelization by tongue and pen had made Gentile Christianity a factor of at least equal importance with Jewish, that our religion was enriched by its Hellenistic strain. The deeper insight into the real significance of Jesus' work and fate born of Paul's peculiar experience and his Hellenistic apprehension of the gospel found embodiment in the beginnings of a New Testament literature. The writings of this period must accordingly be viewed against the background of a critical history. Luke's account, written in the interest of "apostolic" authority, must receive such modifications as the contemporary documents require.

Taking up the story at the point of divergence we see Paul and Barnabas returning to Antioch after the Conference with the Pillars, glad at heart, and expecting now to resume the work for Gentiles without impediment. Besides Titus, John Mark of Jerusalem, a nephew of Barnabas, accompanied them. The Missionary Journey to Cyprus and (southern) Galatia follows, Mark returning, however, to Jerusalem after leaving Cyprus.

It was probably during the absence of the missionaries that "Peter came to Antioch" and, at first, followed the Pauline practice of disregarding 'distinctions of meats.' Later, on arrival of certain "from James" he "drew back and separated himself, fearing those of the circumcision." While matters were at this stage Paul and Barnabas reappeared on the scene. Paul thought it necessary to rebuke Peter "openly, before them all." Barnabas, former head of the Antioch church, took sides with Peter and "the rest of the Jews," doubtless determining the attitude of the church; for Paul says nothing of prevailing upon them by his argument, but merely turns it at once upon the Galatians themselves. Moreover, Barnabas now takes Cyprus as his mission field, with Mark as his helper, while Paul with a new companion, Silvanus (in Acts "Silas," a bearer of the 'decrees' from Jerusalem), takes the northern half of the newly evangelized territory, and through much difficulty and opposition makes his way to the coasts of the Ægean.

This second visit to the churches of Galatia (Acts xvi. 1–5) was signalized by warnings against the (possible) preaching of "another gospel" (Gal. i. 9); for Paul had reason to anticipate trouble from the "false brethren." If Acts may be believed, it was also marked by an extraordinary evidence of Paul's readiness to "become all things to all men" in the interest of conciliation. He is said to have circumcised a Galatian half-Jew named Timothy. If so, it was certainly not to prove his respect for the legal requirement, but rather its indifference. "Circumcision is nothing and uncircumcision nothing; only faith working through love." But these generous 'accommodations' of Paul produced more of misrepresentation than of conciliation. He had cause to regret his liberality later (Gal. i. 10; v. 11 *f*.; *cf*. 1st Cor. vii. 18).

Some unexplained obstacle (Acts xvi. 6) prevented Paul's entrance into the Province of Asia at this time. Ephesus, his probable objective, had perhaps already been occupied (xviii. 24–28). He turned north through Phrygia-Galatia, hoping to find a field in Bithynia, but was again disappointed. At Troas, the very extremity of Asia, came the turning-point in the fortunes of the missionaries. Encouraged by a vision they crossed into Macedonia and found fields white for the harvest.

The Epistles to Thessalonica address one of these Macedonian churches from Corinth, whither the missionaries have been driven. Timothy had been sent back from Athens when Paul's own repeated attempts to return had been frustrated, and has just arrived with good news of the church's perseverance in spite of a persecution stirred up by the Jews. It is against these, apparently, not against Jewish-Christian detractors, that Paul defends his character and message (1st Thess. ii. 1–13). There is also an urgent warning against fornication (iv. 1–8) and exhortation to abound in love (iv. 9–12), with correction of the natural Greek tendency to misapprehend the Jewish eschatology and resurrection-doctrine (iv. 13—v. 1–11; *cf.* 1st Cor. xv.). The closing admonitions relate to the direction of church meetings and discipline.

2nd Thessalonians corrects and supplements the eschatology of 1st Thessalonians by adding a doctrine of Antichrist, which is at all events thoroughly Jewish and earlier than 70, when the temple was destroyed in which it expects the manifestation of "the man of sin." It is the only one of the Epistles of this period whose authenticity is seriously questioned by critical scholarship. How little this affects the question of Paul's 'gospel' may be seen by the fact that the entire contents cover less than 3 per cent. of the earlier Epistles, while the subject is a mere detail.

Far more significant is it to observe the close correspondence between the missionary preaching of Paul as here described by himself (1st Thess. i. 9 *f.*) and the general apostolic message (*kerygma*) as described by Luke (Acts x. 42 *f.*; xiv. 15-17; xvii. 24–31). Where there are no Judaizers there is no reference to the dispensations of Law and Grace and the abolition of the former in the Cross. The doctrine is the common gospel of the Resurrection, wherein Jesus has been manifested as the Messiah. Faith in him secures forgiveness to the repentant; all others are doomed to perish in the judgment shown by his 'manifestation' to be at hand (*cf.* 1st Cor. xv. 11; Rom. i. 3–5).

Galatians was written but slightly before (or after ?) the letters to Thessalonica. Its single theme (after the retrospect) is the Adoption to Sonship through the Spirit. Against the Judaizer's plea that to share in the Inheritance one must be adopted (preferably by circumcision) into the family of Abraham, or at all events pay respect to the Mosaic Law, Paul asserts the single fact of the adoption of the Spirit. "It is because ye are sons that God sent forth the Spirit of his Son into our hearts crying (in the ecstatic utterances of 'tongues') Abba, that is, Father" (Gal. iv. 6). To go back to legal observances is to revert from redemption to bondage. All Christians are indeed sons of Abraham, but only as sharers of his trust in God. Abraham was made "heir of the world" (Rom. iv. 13) for his faith. Circumcision and the Law came afterwards. They were not superimposed stipulations and conditions of the promise. On the contrary they were temporary pedagogic measures intended to produce the consciousness of sin and (moral) death, so that when the Heir should come men should be ready to cast themselves on the mercy of God displayed in his vicarious death.[1] Thus the messianic Redemption is a redemption from a system issuing in sin and death. On the cross even the sinless Christ incurred the curse in order that believers thus redeemed might have the Blessing of the Abrahamic promise (Gal. iii. 1—iv. 7).

But this transfer from bondage to liberty, from the legal to the filial relation, does not "make Christ a minister of sin." On the contrary, if the delivering Spirit of sonship has been received at all, it controls the life for purity and love. One cannot be a son and be unfilial or unbrotherly. The unity of the redeemed world in Christ is the unity of loving service, not of subjection to a bygone

[1] Romans enlarges the conception of the economy of Law by making it include the Gentile law of 'conscience' (Rom. i. 18—ii. 16). In Galatians this point is covered only by classing the "angels" through whom the Mosaic Law was given, with the "Elements" honoured in Gentile religion. Both are codes of "stewards and governors."

system of rules (iv. 8—vi. 18). Thus does Galatians meet the insidious plea of the Judaizers, and their charges against Pauline liberty.

The church founded by Paul in Corinth (Acts xviii. 1–17) was grounded from the beginning in this doctrine of the Cross. Paul purposely restricted himself to it (1st Cor. i. 17–25; ii. 1–5). He had indeed a world-view, of which we learn more in the Epistles of the Captivity, a philosophy revealed by the Spirit as a "mystery of God." Those who afterwards in Corinth came to call themselves followers "of Apollos" had nothing to teach him on this score. But consideration of this Grecizing tendency, too often issuing in a mere "philosophy and vain deceit after the Elements of the world and not after Christ" (Col. ii. 8), must be deferred, in favour of questions which became more immediately pressing. For after Paul had left Corinth to make a brief visit via Ephesus to Cæsarea and Antioch, and had returned through the now pacified Galatian churches to make Ephesus his permanent headquarters (Acts xviii. 18–23), he received disturbing news of conditions in Corinth. Under Apollos (now at Ephesus with Paul) an Alexandrian convert thoroughly indoctrinated with Paul's gospel (Acts xviii. 24–28) the church had flourished, but discussions had subsequently arisen, resulting in a letter to Paul asking his advice on disputed points. Besides this there were moral blemishes. First the factious strife itself, of which Paul has learned from newcomers from Corinth; secondly a case of unpunished incest. A previous letter from Paul (now lost, or but partially preserved in 2nd Cor. vi. 14—vii. 1) had required the church "to have no company with fornicators." The church, making the application general, had pleaded the impracticability of "going out of the world." Paul now explains: "If any man *that is named a brother* be a fornicator . . . with such a one no, not to eat." After further rebuke for litigiousness, and a lack of moral tone, especially in the matter of "fornication" (ch. vi.), Paul takes up seriatim "the things whereof ye wrote." We are chiefly interested in the long section (viii. 1—xi. 1) on "things offered to idols" wherein Paul instructs those who would be imitators of his freedom, but who forget that he has always refused to assert his rights when thereby the 'weak' were stumbled. Moreover fornication is never among the permissible things, nor even the eating of meats offered to idols *at the heathen banquet itself*. Such food is unobjectionable only when it has been sold in the market, and can be eaten without 'offence.'

The other questions related to church meetings for the "Lord's supper" and the exercise of "spiritual gifts." They give opportunity for the development of Paul's noble doctrine of unity through loving service

(xi. 2—xiv. 40). The doctrinal section of 1st Corinthians concludes with a full statement of Paul's doctrine of the resurrection body (called forth by Greek objections to the Jewish). From the items of business at the close we learn that " the collection for the saints " has been under way some time already " in Galatia," and that Paul hopes, after passing through Macedonia, to join the delegation which is to carry the money to Jerusalem (xvi. 1–6).

As it turned out Paul actually followed the itinerary outlined in 1st Cor. xvi. 1–6, but not until after distressing experiences. Timothy, sent (by way of Macedonia, Acts xix. 22) as Paul's representative (iv. 17; xvi. 10 *f.*), was unable to restore order. The opposition to Paul's apostolic authority, treated almost contemptuously in ix. 1–14, grew to alarming proportions. Paul received so direct and personal an affront (either on a hasty visit undertaken in person from Ephesus, or in the person of Timothy) that he despatched a peremptory ultimatum, whose effect he is anxiously waiting to hear when 2nd Corinthians opens with Paul driven out from Ephesus, a refugee in Macedonia (*c.* 55). It is highly probable that the disconnected section appended between 2nd Cor. ix. 15 and the Farewell, is taken from this " grievous " letter written " out of much affliction and anguish of heart with many tears " (2nd Cor. ii. 1–4; vii. 8–16); for it was not only a peremptory demand for punishment of the offender, but also a letter of forced self-commendation. Paul cannot have written in self-commendation on more than one occasion, and he promises not to repeat this in iii. 1 *ff*. We may take 2nd Cor. x.–xiii., then, as representing the "grievous" letter. The opposition emanates from Judaizers who say they are "of Christ," and may therefore be identical with those of 1st Cor. i. 12. But it has grown to proportions which for a time made Paul despair of the church's loyalty. Titus' arrival in Macedonia with news of their restored obedience had been an inexpressible relief (ii. 5–17; vii. 8–16). It remains only to set his 'ministry of the new covenant' once more in contrast with the Mosaic 'ministry of condemnation and death,' including further elucidation of the doctrine of the resurrection body (iii. 1—vi. 10) and to urge generosity in the matter of the collection (chh. viii.–ix.).

The somewhat disordered, but unmistakably genuine material of 2nd Corinthians was probably given out as a kind of residuum of Pauline material long after our 1st Corinthians had been put in circulation, perhaps when renewed strife had caused the church in Rome to intervene through Clement (95), who quotes 1st Corinthians, but shows no knowledge of 2nd Corinthians. The correspondence is not only invaluable to the church for its pæan of love as the invincible, abiding gift of the Spirit (1st Cor. xiii.) and its sublime eulogy of the "ministry of the new covenant," but instructive in the highest degree to the historian. Almost every aspect of Paul's work as missionary, defender of his own independent apostleship and gospel, guide and instructor of developing Gentile-Christian thought, and ardent commissioner for peace with the apostolic community in Syria, is here set forth. The best exposition of the history is the documentary material itself, and conversely.

Romans was written during the peaceful winter at Corinth (55–56) which followed these weeks of tormenting anxiety in Macedonia (Acts xx. 1–3). Paul feels that he has carried the gospel to the very shores of the Adriatic (xv. 19). He is on the point of going to Jerusalem with his great 'offering of the Gentiles,' and has already fixed his eye on Rome and "Spain"! Just as before the First Missionary Journey he forestalled opposition by frankly laying his gospel before the Pillars, so now he lays it before the church in Rome, but most delicately and tactfully, not as though assuming to admonish Christians already "filled with all knowledge and able to admonish one another" (xv. 14), but "that I with you may be comforted in you, each of us by the other's faith" (i. 12). Thus the Epistle is an eirenicon. For Rome was even more than Ephesus had been, a preoccupied territory, though a metropolis of Paul's mission-field. Most of the church are

Paul's sympathizers, but there are many of the 'weak,' who may easily be 'offended.' The letter repeats and enlarges the argument of Galatians for the gospel of Grace, carrying back the promise to Abraham to its antecedent in the fall of Adam, whereby all mankind had passed under the domination of Sin and Death. The function of the Law is again made clear as bringing men to consciousness of this bondage, till it is done away by (mystical) death and resurrection with Christ. In the adoption wrought by the Spirit the whole creation even, groaning since Adam's time under 'vanity,' is liberated in the manifestation of the sons of God. Jesus, glorified at the right hand of God, is the firstfruits of the cosmic redemption (Rom. i.–viii.). Such is Paul's theory of 'evolution.' It is followed by a vindication of God in history. Rom. ix.–xi. exhibits the relation of Jew and Gentile in the process of the redemption. Israel has for the time being been hardened that the Gentiles may be brought in. Ultimately their very jealousy at this result will bring them also to repentant faith.

Paul's sublime exposition of his view of cosmic and historic redemption is followed (as in all the Epistles) by a practical exhortation (chh. xii.–xiv.), the keynote of which is unity through mutual forbearance and loving service. It repeats the Corinthian figure of the members in the body, and the Galatian definition of the 'law of Christ.' Special application is made to the case of the scrupulous who make distinctions of days and of meats. Here, however (xiv. 1—xv. 13), there is no longer need to resist a threatened yoke. Only tenderness and consideration are urged for the over-scrupulous "brother in Christ." It was in this spirit that Paul and his great company of delegates from the churches of the Gentiles went up to Jerusalem (Acts xx. 4—xxi. 17).

CHAPTER IV

PAUL AS PRISONER AND CHURCH FATHER

THE second period of Paul's literary career begins after an interval of several years. This interval is covered indeed, so far as the great events of the Apostle's personal story are concerned, by the last nine chapters of Acts, but exceedingly obscure as respects the fortunes of his mission-field and the occasion for the group of Epistles which come to us after its close. It is barely possible that a fragment or two from the so-called Pastoral Epistles (1st Timothy, 2nd Timothy, Titus), which seem to be compiled long after Paul's death on the basis of some remnants of his correspondence, may have been written shortly after the arrest in Jerusalem and "first defence." In 2nd Tim. iv. 11–18 a journey is referred to from Troas by way of Ephesus which coincides in many respects with that of Acts xx. If the fragment could be taken out from its present setting it might be possible to identify the two; for it is clear from the forecast of Acts xx. 25, 38 that Paul never did revisit this region. The grip of Rome upon her troublesome prisoner was not relaxed until his martyrdom, probably some considerable time before the "great multitude" whom Nero condemned after the conflagration of 64. However, until analysis can dissect out with greater definiteness the genuine elements of the Pastoral Epistles, they cannot be used to throw light upon the later period of Paul's career. A historical background has indeed been created to meet their requirements—a release of Paul, resumption of missionary activities on the coasts of the Ægean, renewed imprisonment in Rome and ultimate martyrdom. But this has absolutely no warrant outside the Pastorals themselves, and is both inconsistent with Acts and open to criticism intrinsically. The story thus created of a release, *second* visitation of the Greek churches, and *second* imprisonment must, therefore, be regarded as fictitious, and the Pastoral Epistles in their present form as products of the post-Pauline age.

It is our task to trace the development among the Greek churches of Christianity conceived as a "revelation of God in Christ," alongside of its development in the 'apostolic' church, until the period of 'catholic' unity and the completed canon. Upon this development the story of Paul's personal fortunes in Acts throws but little light. We merely see that his great peace-making visit to Jerusalem was suddenly interrupted by his arrest in the temple, while engaged in an act of worship undoubtedly intended by him to demonstrate his willingness in the interest of unity to "become as under the Law to them that are under the Law." After this his great delegation from the Gentile churches must have scattered to their homes. Paul remained a prisoner for two years in Cæsarea, and after an adventurous journey covering the ensuing autumn and winter (59–60), spent two more years in less rigid confinement at Rome. We need no hint from his request in 2nd Tim. iv. 13 for "books and parchments" to infer that the years of forced seclusion in Cæsarea were marked by study and meditation; but narrative and inference together convey but little of what we mainly desire to know: the course of religious development in the Pauline churches, as a background for the literature.

On the other hand recent research into religious conditions in the early Empire has removed the principal objections to the authenticity of Philippians, Philemon, Colossians, and even Ephesians. We are far from being compelled to come down to the time of the great Gnostic systems of the second century to find a historical situation appropriate to this group of letters purporting to be written by Paul from his captivity. Indeed they exhibit on any theory of their origin a characteristic and legitimate development of the Pauline gospel of sonship by the Spirit of Adoption abolishing the dispensation of

Law. It is a development almost inevitable in a conception of 'the gospel' formed on Greek ideas of Redemption, if we place in opposition to it a certain baser type of superstitious, mongrel Judaism, revealed in the Epistles themselves, repeatedly referred to in Acts, and now known to us by a mass of extraneous documentary material.

The new disturbers of the churches' peace revealed in the Epistles of the Captivity are still of Jewish origin and tendency; but at least in the region of Colossæ (in the Lycus Valley, adjacent to southern Galatia) the issue is no longer that between Law and Grace, but concerns the nature and extent of the Redemption. The trouble still comes from a superstitious exaltation of the Mosaic revelation; but those whom Paul here opposes do not "use the Law lawfully," frankly insisting on its permanent obligation as the will of God for all sons, unaffected by the Cross. It is now admitted to be an "ordinance of angels"; but the observance of it is inculcated because man's redemption can only come through conciliation of these higher beings. Mystical union with superhuman Powers is to be promoted by its observances. This superstition is neither purely Jewish, nor purely Greek. It is composite—Hellenistic. Judaism is imitated in the superstitious reverence for the Law; but the conception of Redemption leaves behind every thought of national particularism and is openly individualistic. The redemption sought is that of the individual soul from the limitations of humanity, and doubtless the name of Jesus played an important rôle in the emancipation, as in the exorcisms of the sons of Sceva (Acts xix. 13 *f.*); only it was not "above every name."

But even Jewish apocalypses such as *Enoch* and *Baruch* with all their superstitious angelology and demonology manage somehow to cling to the ancient Jewish faith in the primacy of man, and Paul in like manner upholds against the theosophists the doctrine of the believer's sonship and joint-heirship with Christ. In fact the Adoption, Redemption and Inheritance accorded in the gift of the Spirit are to his mind gifts so great and exalted as to make it a "gratuitous self-humiliation" to pay homage, in Mosaic or other ceremonial, to "angels," "principalities," or "powers." In Christ we already have a foothold in the heavenly regions. We were foreordained in his person to be "heirs" "before the foundation of the world." His resurrection and ascension "to the right hand of God" participated in by us through "the Spirit" was a "triumph" over the 'Elements' and 'Rulers.' They should be beneath the Christian's feet in feeling, as they soon will be in reality.

This exalted doctrine of Christ's sonship as compared with the mere temporary authority of "angels and principalities and powers," secures to the Epistles of the Captivity their well-deserved title of "Christological"; for they lay the foundation for all later doctrines of the Logos or Word. It is well to realize, however, that the doctrine is in origin and meaning simply a vindication of the divine dignity of manhood.

An idea of outward conditions at the time of writing may be gained from the two Epistles of the group most universally admitted to be genuine, Philemon and Philippians. Both are written from captivity, almost certainly in Rome, because the writer is expecting, if released, to revisit the Ægean coasts, which was not Paul's expectation in Cæsarea. But there is a wide difference between the two as respects the circumstances presupposed. The tone of Philemon is hopeful, sprightly, even jocose. Paul is in company with a group of "fellow-workers" which significantly includes "Mark," as well as two companions of the voyage to Rome, "Aristarchus" of Thessalonica, and "Luke" (Acts xxvii. 2). Epaphras, his "fellow-prisoner," appears in Colossians as the founder of that church and a teacher in the adjacent towns of Hierapolis and Laodicea. He has brought to Paul either of his own knowledge or by report from others, disturbing news of the inroads of the heresy. Onesimus, whose case occasions the letter to Philemon, is an escaped slave of this friend and convert of Paul. The apostle is sending back the slave with the request that he be forgiven and manumitted. The interrelation of the persons mentioned in Philemon and Colossians shows that the occasion is the same. Tychicus (*cf.* Acts xx. 3) the bearer of Colossians (Col. iv. 7) accompanies Onesimus. Ephesians (if authentic) belongs to the same group, being also carried by Tychicus (Eph. vi. 21). It was certainly *not* intended for Ephesus, but for some church or churches not directly known to Paul (i. 15; iii. 2). It bears much the same relation to Colossians as Romans to Galatians. In spite of copious evidences of its use reaching back even to Clement of Rome (95) the genuineness of Ephesians is more seriously questioned than that of any other Pauline letter save the Pastorals. In the present writer's judgment this suspicion is unfounded, but the question of Pauline, semi-Pauline or deutero-Pauline is immaterial to the general development.

Philippians is of later date than Philemon and its companions. Paul has been in circumstances of dire physical distress, and is comforting his correspondents in view of an immediately impending decision of his case (ii. 23). The issue will be life or death, and Paul has no earthly (but only super-earthly) reasons for hoping the verdict may not be adverse. He is still expecting, if released, to revisit the Ægean coast (ii. 24); but it is only smiling through his tears when he tells the Philippians that their need of him is so great that he is confident he will be spared to them (Phil. 1. 12–30). Knowing that this journey was never made, we can but infer that the fate so near at hand in Phil. ii. 17 came actually to pass. Paul's blood was "poured out a libation," as tradition of extreme antiquity credibly reports, and it can hardly have been after a release, return to Greece and second arrest. The passage in 2nd Tim iv. 5–8 which repeats the figure of the libation (Phil. ii. 17), treating it no longer as doubtful, but a tragic certainty, will have been penned (if authentic) but a few weeks at most after Philippians, and immediately before the end. If Philemon-Colossians-Ephesians be dated in 62, Philippians, with the possible fragments in 2nd Timothy, may be dated a few months later.

Conditions at Philippi appear only in a favourable light from this latest authentic epistle. Paul can thank God upon every remembrance of these loyal and liberal Macedonian friends. In Rome, however, he is still affected by Judaizing opposition, though his attitude toward it (in Rome at least) shows the significant difference from Galatians that he can now be thankful that Christ is preached even thus (Phil i. 15–18). Moreover there is a difference in the type of legalism represented; for while in his warning to the Philippians of the possible coming of the heretics Paul is moved to recall his own renunciation of legalistic righteousness, the terms of opprobrium applied to the disturbers imply an immorality and assimilation to heathenism (Phil. iii. 2 19; *cf.* Rom. xvi. 17–20) which could not justly be said to characterize the legalism of the synagogue.

The doctrinal elements of Philippians consist of two passages: (1) the denunciation of the "concision" (a term applied to the heathenized renegade Jew) ending with a reminder of the high enthronement of our spiritual Redeemer (iii. 1–21); (2) the definition of the "mind," or "disposition," of Christ exhibited in his self-abnegating incarnation, obedient suffering, and supreme exaltation (ii. 5–11). Both passages are characteristic of Paul's gospel in general, which is always, as against that of the Judaizers, the gospel of a drama, or spectacle, witnessed; not a gospel of teachings heard. It is a gospel *about* Jesus, not of precepts inculcated *by* Jesus, a drama of redemption for all mankind out of servitude into sonship, wherein the cross is central. Both passages are also characteristic, as we shall see, of the later period of Paul's literary activity; for even in Philippians, the dominant doctrinal motive is the Redemption to which Paul is looking forward, and this is now conceived even more strongly than in the earlier letters in terms of personal religion. He anticipates "departing to be with Christ" (i. 23) rather than awaiting Him on earth (1st Thess. iv. 17). The "goal" toward which the Christian "presses on" is personal immortality through mystic union with Christ in the life of God (iii. 10–14). This too is a real doctrine of the Kingdom of God; but its starting-point is humanity's triumph over its enemies 'sin' and 'death,' not Israel's triumph over its oppressors. Still more in the Colossian group does it become apparent how the 'far-off, divine event' is a unity of mankind through the Spirit corresponding to the Stoic figure of the members and the body rather than the 'Kingdom of David.'

Again the opponents in Phil. iii. 2, 18 *f*. are not mere Pharisaic legalists, unable to see that Law and Grace are mutually exclusive systems, and nullifying the significance of the Cross by perpetuating the system it was intended to abolish. If we may explain the difference by Colossians, they are Jews of heathenish tendencies, pretended adherents of the gospel, who nullify its significance by perpetuating regard for the Law; only the servility deplored is not servility toward God, but toward "angels" (Col. ii. 18).

To appreciate the enlargement which has come to Christianity beyond its merely 'apostolic' form through the independent development of the Greek churches in this second period we must realize that Paul's 'gospel of the uncircumcision' differed in respect to promise as well as law. The coming Kingdom which he preached was something more than "the kingdom of our father

David" extended from Jerusalem. What it really was becomes fully apparent only in the 'Christological Epistles.' But we must study the opposition to appreciate how differently the idea of Redemption had developed on Greek soil.

That aspect of Judaism which was most conspicuous to the outsider in Paul's day was not the legalism of the scribes and the Palestinian synagogue, perpetually embalmed in the Talmud and orthodox rabbinism of to-day. It was the superstition and magic which excite the contempt of satirists like Horace, Juvenal, and Martial, and call forth descriptions like that of the letter of Hadrian to Servianus, characterizing the Samaritans, Jews *and Christians* dwelling in Egypt as "all astrologers, haruspices, and quacksalvers." It is this type of Jew who is most widely known in the contemporary Hellenistic world; whose spells and incantations, framed in Old Testament language, are perpetuated in the leaden incantation rolls and magic papyri of the Berlin collection; whose portrait is painted in the Simon Magus of Acts viii. 14–24, the Elymas the sorcerer of Acts xiii. 6–12, the "strolling Jews, exorcists," and the "seven sons of Sceva" of Acts xix. 13–20. A Christian writer early in the second century is so impressed with this characteristic of contemporary Judaism that he even distinguishes as the third type of religion, besides idolatry and Christianity, "the Jews, who fancy that they alone know God, but do not, worshipping angels and archangels, the moon and the month," and seeks to prove his case by citing the Old Testament festal system. Indeed this idea of Judaism is the predominant one among the second-century apologists. Jewish "superstition" is a notorious fact of the time. The transcendentalizing of Jewish theology after the Persian period had led inevitably to an elaborate angelology and demonology. When as part of this process a more and more supernatural character was attributed to the Law it could but have a twofold effect. The learned and orthodox would treat it soberly as a revelation of the divine will. This is the legalistic development we see in the Talmud and the Palestinian synagogue. The ignorant and superstitious, especially in the Greek-speaking world, would use it as a book of magic. This is what we see among many Jewish sects, particularly in Samaria, Egypt and among the Greek-speaking Jews. The tendency was marked even in Galilee. Jesus Himself stigmatizes the morbid craving of His countrymen for miracles as the mark of an "adulterous" generation, because the power invoked was not divine, but always angelic, or even demonic. Paul alludes to the same trait (1st Cor. i. 22). But while there is a singular absence both from the Pauline and the Johannine writings of any reference to exorcism, the typical miracle of Synoptic story, it has been justly remarked that no element of Paul's thought has been so little affected by that of Jesus as his angelology and demonology. Paul's world-view, like that of the apocalypses of his time, is a perfect phantasmagoria of angels and demons, "gods many and lords many." His conception of the redemption conflict is not a wrestling against flesh and blood, but against "world-rulers of this (lower region of) darkness," against "archangels," "elements," "principalities," "powers." The one thing which takes away all harmful influence from this credulity (if we must apply an unfairly modern judgment to an ancient writer) is his doctrine of the Sonship and Lordship of Jesus, with whom the redeemed are "joint-heirs" of the entire creation and thus superior to angels. In this respect Paul has imbibed the mind of Christ. Jesus' remedy for superstition is not scientific but religious. It does not deny the popularly assumed relation to "spirits" good or evil, but affirms a direct relation to the Infinite Spirit, which reduces all angels and demons to insignificance save as "ministers." Paul's world-view starts with the creation of man to be lord and heir of the world (Gal. iv. 1; 1st Cor. iii. 22; *cf.* Gen. i. 28). The "purpose of God, which he purposed in Christ Jesus, before the creation, unto a dispensation of the fulness of the ages" is "to our glory." It would be frustrated if the "Second Adam" did not become the

Heir, in whom the redeemed creation would find the goal of its long expectancy. Paul has a cosmology as well as "Enoch." He could not be a worthy follower of Jesus—he could not even be a loyal "son of the Law" without holding to the accepted doctrine of the Inheritance intended for Messiah and his obedient people. It did not make him less firm in this conviction when as a Christian he thought of Jesus as the Messiah, and of Jew and Gentile united in his kingdom; only the starting-point is not the subjection of the sons of Abraham under Gentiles, but the subjection of the sons of Adam under "world-rulers of this darkness." When he combines Ps. viii. and Ps. cx. in his depiction of the reign of Christ in 1st Cor. xv. 24–27, it is a sure indication of its scope as Paul understood it. He included in the lordship over creation, and the subjection of all "enemies" which the exalted Christ is awaiting "at the right hand of God," the subjection of "angels, and principalities, and powers and every name that is named, whether of beings in heaven, or on earth, or under the earth." Paul pursues, then, the method of the apocalyptic writers in making his doctrine of Redemption and the Kingdom transcendental. By making it cosmic he undermines its Jewish particularism. He avoids the superstition by holding firmly to Jesus' doctrine of sonship by *moral* affinity with God.

In the Christological Epistles accordingly

it is apparent that the Pauline churches are learning to think of the coming Kingdom in a widely different way from the 'apostolic.' The Greek doctrine of mystic union, not the rabbinic of a "share in the world to come," is the basis. In due time we shall see how difficult the process of reconciliation became between Greek and Semitic thought in this field also. For the present we can only note how in the great theme of the Unity of the Spirit in Eph. iv. 1—vi. 9 it is not the 'apostolic' ideal of a restoration of the kingdom to Israel according to the oath sworn to Abraham (Luke i. 68–75; *cf.* Acts i. 6) that dominates, but an enlargement of the figure of the body and members, a figure commonly employed by Stoic writers, to apply to the unity of the church in Corinthians and Romans. In the Epistles of the Captivity the doctrine of the Kingdom is a social organism permeated and vitalized by Christ's spirit of service. Personal immortality is union with the life of God.

In view of the notoriety of Ephesus as the very centre of the trade in magic (so much so that spells and incantations were technically known as "Ephesian letters") and of what Acts tells us of the enormous destruction there of "books of magic" effected by Paul's preaching, it is not surprising that Asia and Phrygia should appear a few years after Paul's departure as the hot-bed of a "philosophy and vain deceit, after the tradition of men, after the 'elements' of the world, and not after Christ." Acts xx. 29 makes Paul predict the heresy.

Such was especially the case at Colossæ, a little town long after notorious for its superstition, where Epaphras, now Paul's fellow-prisoner, had founded the church. Epaphras himself at the time of Paul's writing was in great anxiety both for this church and for the adjoining churches at Hierapolis and Laodicea. Colossians is written to meet this danger, and was sent by the same bearers as the note to Philemon. It was to be exchanged, after being read at Colossæ, for another epistle sent simultaneously to Laodicea. Whether our Ephesians is this companion letter or only a deutero-Pauline production framed on the basis of some genuine letter written on this occasion, is a disputed point among critics. In Marcion's canon our Ephesians was called "Laodiceans," and in our own oldest textual authorities it has no address. We may assume that Ephesians is really the companion letter, whose original address was for some reason cancelled;[1] or that it is but partially from Paul's own hand. Neither view will materially alter our conception of his teaching, or the special application of it to the circumstances of the

[1] Harnack very ingeniously suggests as a reason the ill repute later incurred by Laodicea (*cf.* Rev. iii. 15 *f.*); comparing the chiselling out from inscriptions of the names of unpopular kings.

churches of the Lycus Valley. The important thing to observe is that whereas the application in Colossians is specific, in Ephesians it is systematic and general. Colossians wages a direct polemic against those who are making believers the spoil of mere 'Elements' by introducing distinctions of "meats *and drinks*" (a step beyond Mosaism), with observance of "feast days, new moons and sabbaths." In Ephesians we have, either altogether at first hand, or to a greater or less extent at second, a general, affirmative presentation of Paul's doctrine of Lordship in Christ. It has only incidental allusion to being "deceived with empty words" (v. 6), and a warning not to be "children tossed to and fro and carried about with every wind of doctrine, by the sleight of men in craftiness, after the wiles of error" (iv. 14).

Colossians and Ephesians develop, accordingly, that (cosmological) wisdom of God conveyed to Paul by the Spirit of Christ in a "mystery," at which he had only hinted in 1st Cor. ii. 1–16. Paul's *gnosis*, or insight, concerns the purpose of God in creation, hidden even from the (angelic) "world-rulers," who are coming to nought. The Spirit of Christ, who as the divine Wisdom had been the agent of creation, is given to Christian apostles and prophets. It affords them in the revelation of this "mystery" a philosophy both of creation and redemption which puts to shame mere speculative reasoning. The Inheritance—the things God prepared for those that love Him—consists (as an apocalyptic writer had said) of "things which eye had not seen, nor ear heard, nor had entered into the heart of man to conceive."[1] Paul had purposely refrained from unfolding this revealed cosmology and philosophy of history to the Corinthians, in order to avoid just the evils which the teaching of Apollos had apparently precipitated at the time when 1st Corinthians was written. Still, we can gain from this very epistle (1st Cor. viii. 6; xv. 24–28) a partial conception of his doctrine of Christ as the beginning and end of the creation, the Wisdom of God by whom and for whom as Heir, all things were created. From Romans i.–viii. and ix.–xi. we can easily see that as Second Adam the Messiah was to Paul the key to the world's development and to human history; for since the triumph of Satan in Eden the whole creation had waited, groaning, for the advent of the sons. Galatians makes it no less clear that he thought of the Cross as the epoch-making event, which marks the transition from the period of the control of the world by secondary agencies, to the rule of the Son. This "mystery" is simply brought out and developed now in the Epistles of the Captivity. The effort and prayer is that the readers may "have the eyes of their heart enlightened,"[2] obtain something of Paul's own insight into the riches of the inheritance they are to share with Christ, something of Paul's experience of the power of God in raising Christ from the dead and setting Him on the throne of glory. If they but realize what sonship and heirship with Christ implies—if they but take in the fact that by the resurrection Spirit within them they have already in a sense shared in this deliverance and this exaltation, they will be forearmed against all the vain deceits of theosophy. It is in fact this resurrection Spirit which brings about the unity of the world as a single organism. It extends from the uppermost height to the nethermost abyss. And because it is the Spirit of Jesus, it fills all it touches with the disposition to loving service. It affords a new ethics and a new politics whose keynote is the law of love in imitation of God and Christ. All social relations are recreated by it, beginning with family and church. Hence we must think of our redemption as like Israel's from the bondage and darkness of Egypt. The principalities and powers of this world, spiritual hosts of wickedness in the superterrestrial regions, are vainly endeavouring to hold back the people of God, in "this darkness." We have only to wait like Israel at the Passover "with our loins girt, and our feet shod." The Deliverer will soon appear from heaven, clad in armour of salvation, as in the ancient passover songs, cleaving the darkness with his sword of light, and leading forth the captives.

In these themes, variously interwoven in Ephesians and Colossians, it is difficult to say whether it is the note of unity or the note of freedom which predominates. Certainly we can recognize the same great apostle of liberty who in the epistles of the earlier period had proved the power and value of his religious insight by seizing upon the doctrine of sonship as the essential heart of the gospel. It is the same genius consciously taught of God who had demanded and obtained recognition on equal terms for his gospel of Grace and sonship, a gospel given by revelation of God's Son "in" him, who now demands that the gift of the Spirit to Jew and Gentile be recognized as calling for reconstruction of the doctrine of the coming Kingdom. "He that ascended is the same also that descended to the lowest depths that he might fill all things." And he poured out the "gifts" in order that they might make one organism of the new social order, a new creation animated and vitalized by Jesus' spirit of loving service.

For just as in all the great earlier epistles the note of longing for peace and unity in love rings ever stronger and clearer above the strife, so in the later epistles, the note of triumph in liberty has a deep under-chord of thanksgiving for reconciliation achieved. The great pæan of reverent adoration for the glory of God's grace in Eph. i. 3–14, is a thanksgiving for the union of Jew and Gentile in one common redemption. The retrospect of the work of God in ii. 11–21 is the proclamation of "peace to him that was far off and peace to him that was nigh." It is described as the building of Jew and Gentile into one living temple, upon the foundation of the apostles and prophets, Christ Jesus Himself being the chief corner-stone. The exhortation to the unity of the Spirit in iv. 1—vi. 9 rests upon an exultant application of the figure of the "one new man" in whose body all are members, that would be inconceivable if at the time of writing the church which had received the gifts from the ascended Lord was not indeed one body, but two bodies standing apart in mutual distrust and jealousy.

In fact we may say not of Ephesians only, but of Colossians likewise, and indeed of all the group: Their keynote is not so much the conquest of all things by Christ as "the reconciliation of all things in Christ, whether things upon the earth, or things in the heavens" (Col. i. 20). It is not unreasonable to infer from such undertones as these that the prayer was answered in which Paul when he set out from Corinth had besought the Roman church by our Lord Jesus Christ and by the love of the Spirit to strive together with him, that his ministration which he had for Jerusalem might be acceptable to the saints, that so his coming to them in Rome through the will of God might be in joy, and that together with them he might find rest.

CHAPTER V

PSEUDO-APOSTOLIC EPISTLES

WE cannot wonder that an epoch of the church's history which followed upon the martyrdom in rapid succession of all its remaining great leaders, should at first be poor in literary products. James the Lord's brother was stoned to death by a mob in Jerusalem in the year 61–2. His namesake, brother of John, had been beheaded early in 44 by Herod Agrippa I. Among the "others" who, as Josephus informs us, perished along with James in 61, we may, perhaps, reckon John, who stands beside him in Paul's list of the Pillars. This John, son of Zebedee, brother of the other James, is reckoned a martyr in the same sense as his brother in the earliest gospels. The brothers are assured that they shall drink the same cup of suffering as the Lord, though they may not claim in return pre-eminent seats in glory (Mark x. 39 *f*.). John did not suffer with his brother James in 44, because he is present at the conference in 46–7 (Gal. ii. 9); but one of the traditions of the Jerusalem elders reported by Papias declared that he was "killed by the

Jews" in fulfilment of the Lord's prediction, and this early tradition must be accepted in spite of its conflict with one which gradually superseded it after John came to be regarded as author of Revelation and the Fourth Gospel. The statement that he was killed "together with James his brother" may be due merely to the (not infrequent) confusion of the two Jameses.

Paul's decapitation in Rome occurred not more than a year or two later, and was followed there in 64, according to very ancient and trustworthy tradition, by the martyrdom of Peter. The death of all the principal leaders explains why the Jerusalem church when it reassembled after the overthrow of city and temple in the year 70, put forward no more prominent candidates for the leadership than a certain Symeon, son of Clopas, one of the group of 'relatives of the Lord' who are traceable "until the time of Trajan," and a certain unknown Thebuthis. Symeon, according to Eusebius, who takes his account from Hegesippus (165), was the representative of "those of the apostles and disciples of the Lord that were still living, together with the Lord's relatives." Thebuthis is said to have sprung from one of the heretical Jewish sects and to have organized a schism in consequence of his disappointment. All we can be sure of is that Jerusalem 'down to the time of Trajan' continued to regard itself as the seat of apostolic authority and arbiter of orthodoxy, on account of its succession of disciples and relatives of the Lord. Among the latter the leading, if not the only, representatives of the seed of David, when " search was made " in the persecution under Domitian (81–95), were two *grandsons* of Jude, the Lord's brother. Jude himself, then, was no longer living. Luke (*c.* 100), Papias (145), and Hegesippus (165) successively exhibit the growing authority of the " tradition handed down," especially that of " the apostles and elders in Jerusalem." But what Papias records of the traditions of these " elders " does not rise above the level of Jewish midrash, and the epistles which bear the names of James and Jude have little intrinsic value, and enjoyed from the beginning only the most meagre acceptance. At Rome tradition attaches to the name of Peter, but besides the bare fact of his martyrdom " at the same time with Paul " (64–5) it has little of value to relate. We cannot safely go beyond the tradition reported by Porphyry that Peter fed the lambs (at Rome) for a few months before his martyrdom, and that reported by Papias that Mark, who had been Peter's assistant, compiled there the Gospel which bears his name, basing it upon his recollections of Peter's preaching. Of this vitally important work (*c.* A.D. 75) we must speak in another connection. We are concerned at present with writings which directly reflect the development of Christian life and doctrine in this sub-apostolic period, especially that in the Pauline mission-field.

Except for the appearance of the Gospel of Mark at Rome (*c.* 75) there remains nothing to break the silence and darkness of twenty years after the deaths of James and Peter and Paul. The writings which finally did appear were almost inevitably anonymous or pseudepigraphic, because apostolic authority stood so high that no other could secure circulation. Hebrews (*c.* 85) has an epistolary attachment at the close of its "exhortation," but either never had an address or superscription, or else has been deprived of it. All the Synoptic writings are anonymous, though Luke–Acts (*c.* 100) is dedicated to a literary patron. Revelation (*c.* 95) is boldly asserted to be the work of the Apostle John in the prefatory chapters and the epilogue (i. 2, 4, 9; xxii. 8). But the body of the work, though of Palestinian origin, has a totally different standpoint, and claims the authority of a prophet, not that of an apostle. Similarly the Fourth gospel when finally published received an appendix (ch. xxi.) which cautiously suggests the Apostle John as its author; but the three Epistles by the same writer are anonymous. The homily called James (90–100) has a superscription which superficially connects it with the chief authority in Jerusalem, and the Epistle of Jude prefixes to itself the name which stood next in the same class. But even in antiquity they had a precarious standing, and neither is a real letter. Finally there are the Epistles to Timothy and Titus, purporting to be written by Paul, and a whole series of every kind, epistles, gospel, acts, and apocalypse, written in the name of Peter, of which only two secured final adoption into the canon. Of all these only 1st Peter and the so-called Pastoral Epistles (1st and 2nd Timothy and Titus) have some claim to be considered genuine; for 1st Peter is certainly of early origin (*c.* 85), and was undisputed in antiquity; while the Pastorals, though rejected by Marcion, and as a whole of late date (90–110), are made up on the basis of some authentic Pauline material.

The post-apostolic epistles may be grouped into two classes, according as they are predominantly occasioned (*a*) by internal dangers of heresy and moral laxity; or (*b*) by the external peril of persecution. To the former (*a*) must be reckoned (1) the so-called Pastoral Epistles; (2) Jude; (3) 2nd Peter. All these concern themselves outspokenly with a type of false doctrine which has certain more or less definite traits, and is tending toward the Gnostic heresies of the second century, if not yet clearly identifiable with them. But the inspired genius of Paul is wanting. The age is not creative, but conservative. Its writers are ecclesiastics and church teachers, not apostles and prophets. Their distinctive note is appeal to apostolic authority. Whether the name by which they cover their own insignificance be that of "Paul," or "Jude the brother (son ?) of James," or "Peter," they have little or no independent message. They hark back to the "pattern of sound words" the "deposit," "the faith once for all delivered to the saints," "the words spoken before by the holy prophets, and the commandments of the Lord and Saviour through your apostles," in particular the "wisdom of our beloved brother Paul" who (in the Pastoral Epistles) had predicted the heresy, and "in all his epistles" had spoken of the resurrection and judgment. Second Peter, which refers in the passage just quoted (2nd Pet. iii. 2, 15 *f.*) to the Pauline Epistles alongside "the other Scriptures" belongs to a very late period (*c.* 150). In fact this Epistle, now almost universally recognized to be pseudonymous, merely reëdits the Epistle of Jude, supplying a prefix (ch. i.) and an appendix (ch. iii.) to make special application of its denunciations to the case of the false teachers who were "denying the (bodily) resurrection and the judgment." Neither plagiarism nor pseudonymity were recognized offences at the time; so that we bring no indictment against the author of 2nd Peter, were he the Apostle or not. Still our conception of the Galilean fisherman will be higher without this example of pulpit rhetoric than with it.

Of the nature of the heresies controverted in this series of writings we must speak later.

As to the region whence they originate something can be made out already. Not indeed from 2nd Peter, which is of too late date to be of service. True the readers addressed are assumed to be the same as in the first epistle, in other words the Pauline mission-field of Asia Minor (1st Pet. i. 1), and there is reason to think " Asia " was the region first affected. " Ephesus " and " Asia " are in fact the regions affected in 1st and 2nd Timothy (1st Tim. i. 3 *f.*; 2nd Tim. i. 15). Moreover it is in this same region that we find Polycarp (110–117) adverting to those who " pervert the sayings of the Lord to their own lusts, and deny the resurrection and judgment." To the same region and the same period belong the letters of " the Spirit " in Rev. i.–iii. (*c.* 95) with their denunciation of the Balaamite and Nicolaitan heretics, and still further 1st–3rd John and the Epistles of Ignatius, which are also polemics against a Gnostic heresy (Doketism) tending to moral laxity. It is doubtful, however, in view of the general address (2nd Pet. i. 1), whether the author of 2nd Peter really has a definite circle in mind, and does not rather in iii. 1 mistakenly treat 1st Peter as a general epistle. Denial of the resurrection and judgment was not limited to one locality or period. Hegesippus regards it as a pre-Christian heresy combated already by James. Equally precarious would be the assumption that Jude, with its similar general address, was necessarily intended for Asia Minor. The false teachers resemble those we know of there, and the denunciation is incorporated by 2nd Peter, but 'Cainites' and 'Balaamites' were not confined to the regions of 1st John and Revelation, and Jude might have almost any date between 90 and 120. The most that can be said is that before the death of Paul the last view we obtain of his mission-field shows it exposed, especially in the region of Ephesus, to a rising flood of superstition and false doctrine, while documents that can be dated with some definiteness in 95–117, such as Revelation, the Johannine and Ignatian Epistles, and the letter of Polycarp, show a great advance of heretical teaching in the same region. The later heresy corresponds in several respects to that combatted in the Pastorals, Jude and 2nd Peter, but becomes at last more distinctly definable as Doketism, whose most obnoxious form comes to be denial of the (bodily) resurrection and judgment. The three Pastoral Epistles, Jude and 2nd Peter may, therefore, be taken as probably reflecting the growing internal danger confronted by the churches of Asia (if not by all the churches) in the sub-apostolic age.

Unfortunately, literary relations sometimes interfere with historical classification, and we are, therefore, compelled to defer treatment of 1st–3rd John and the Epistles of "the Spirit" to the churches (Rev. i. 3), which really belong to our present group (*a*) of writings against the heresies of (proconsular) Asia. Their relation to the special canon of Ephesus, whose writings are all ascribed to John, makes it convenient to consider them in another connection. The reader should bear in mind, however, that the group extends continuously down to the Epistles of Ignatius and centres upon Ephesus, where, according to Acts xx. 29 *f.*, the "grievous wolves" were to enter in after Paul's departing.

Similar considerations affect the grouping of the Epistle of James, which almost demands a class by itself. It might be called anti-heretical, except that its nature is the reverse of controversial, and its author seems to have no direct contact with the false teachers. In a remote and general way he deplores the vain talk and disputation which go hand in hand with a relaxation of the practical Christian virtues. On the whole it seems more correct to class James with 1st Peter and Hebrews, particularly as it displays direct literary dependence on the former, if not on both.

Our second group (*b*) consists of writings not primarily concerned with heresy. Its first and best example speaks in the name of Peter as representative of "apostolic" Christianity at Rome. But the doctrine, and even the phraseology and illustrations of 1st Peter are largely borrowed from the greater Epistles of Paul, particularly Romans and Ephesians.

Nothing even remotely suggests an author who had enjoyed personal relations with Jesus, or could relate his wonderful words and deeds. On the contrary the doctrine is Paul's gospel minus the sting of the abolition of the Law. In view of the known internal conditions of the churches to which 1st Peter is addressed in Pontus, Galatia, Cappadocia, *Asia* and Bithynia it is remarkable how completely the subject of heresy or false doctrine is ignored. Their adversary the devil is not at present taking the form of a seducing serpent (2nd Cor. xi. 3), but of a "roaring lion" openly destroying and devouring (1st Pet. v. 8 *f*.), and the same sufferings the Asiatics are called upon to endure are being inflicted upon their brethren throughout the world. A systematic, universal "fiery persecution" is going on, which has come almost as a surprise (iv. 12) and may compel any believer, after having made "defence" before the magistrate of "the hope that is in him," to "suffer as a Christian" and to "glorify God in this name." The author exhorts to irreproachable conduct as citizens, and kindness and good order in the brotherhood. If such blamelessness of living be combined with patient endurance of the unjust punishment, Christians who still must sanctify in their hearts Christ (and not the Emperor) as Lord, will ultimately be left unharmed.

Superior as is this noble exhortation to patient endurance of suffering in the meekness of Christ to the controversial rhetoric of 2nd Peter, immeasurably better as is its attestation in ancient and modern times, even the most conservative modern critics are compelled to regard it as at least semi-pseudonymous. It might be just possible to carry back the conditions of persecution presupposed to the time of Nero. But if it be Peter writing from Rome after the recent martyrdoms of James and Paul, why is there no allusion to either? Again, we might possibly prolong the life of Peter (against all probability) down to the beginning of the reign of Domitian (81–95). In that case the absence of any allusion to the great events of recent occurrence in Palestine would be almost equally hard to explain. Moreover, with any dating the real author remains a literary man, a Paulinist, a Grecian Jew, and the share attributable to Peter personally becomes most shadowy. The simpler, and (as the present writer has come to believe) the more probable view is that 1st Peter, like the later writings which assumed the name, is wholly pseudonymous. If, however, it appeared (as we are persuaded) some twenty years after the Apostle's death, among those perfectly aware of the fact, assuming no other disguise, but frankly dealing with the existing situation, this is a kind of pseudonymity which should be classed with literary fictions and conventions which are harmless because (at the time) perfectly transparent. Letters written under fictitious names were in fact a very common literary device of the age.

At all events the Apostle appears as an old man (v. 1) writing from "Babylon"—rightly taken by the fathers to be a cryptogram for Rome. Salutations are conveyed from Mark, his "son" (*cf.* Philem. i. 10). The bearer (writer ?) is represented to be Silvanus (like Mark a companion of Paul with relations to Jerusalem as well), and Silvanus is commended as a "trustworthy" disciple. The author states it as his object to "exhort and testify that this is the true grace of God wherein ye stand."

Ignorant as we are of its author's name it is fortunate for our study of the times that the date of 1st Peter is fairly determinable by the convergence of external and internal evidence. Echoes from it appear already in Clement of Rome (95) as well as in James and Hermas. We must think of it, then, as a hand of cordial encouragement extended by a representative of the Petro-Pauline church at Rome, soon after the outbreak of the persecution of Domitian (*c.* 90), to the still independent but suffering churches of Asia Minor. If we remember that it undertakes to endorse the doctrine of one third of contemporary Christendom, and (in substance) offers a 'letter of commendation' to Silvanus, it will be obvious that no name of less authority than that of Peter could have served. As Zahn has well remarked: "The significant thing . . . is that it is Peter, the most distinguished apostle of the circumcision (Gal. ii. 7) who bears witness to the genuineness of their state of grace."

We must place alongside of 1st Peter one other epistle in which the motive of exhortation to endurance of persecution without relaxation of the moral standard is prominent, though not exclusive, and a second, wherein it appears only in a faint echo of "trials," which turn out, however, as the reader proceeds, to be only "temptations," while the real occasion of writing is plain—moral relaxation without either heresy or persecution to excuse it. The two writings in question are the anonymous "exhortation" handed down under the title "To the Hebrews," and the so-called Epistle (in reality a homily) of James. Hebrews begins as an exposition of the two psalms Paul had quoted in his reference in 1st Cor. xv. 24–28 to the exaltation of Jesus (Pss. viii. and cx.) proving Him to be the Son, who, after temporary subordination to the angels, has been exalted above them to the place of supreme dominion. Christ has thus effected a greater redemption than Moses and Joshua. He is also a "high-priest after the order of Melchizedek" according to Ps. cx.; so that the Aaronic priesthood and ceremonial are surpassed as well as the Mosaic legislation, by the sacrifice of Calvary and intercession of the risen Redeemer. It is no wonder that in the period of debate against Judaism the canon-makers gave to this anonymous sermon a title which ranks it first in the class of subsequent controversial pamphlets "against the Jews." Controversy, however, is subordinate in the writer's purpose to edification. He is not unconscious of the dangers of that superstitious 'worship of the angels,' against which Paul's Asian epistles had been directed, but his demonstration of the superiority of the institutions and aims of Christianity to those of Judaism has the practical object of reinforcing the courage and "faith" of his readers under pressure of persecution. His argument culminates in an inspiring list of Scriptural heroes and martyrs, leading up as a climax to "Jesus the author and perfecter of our faith." As Jesus endured, looking beyond the shame and suffering of the cross to the joy of His reward, so should the readers "endure their chastening." Apostacy will meet a fearful doom in the judgment of fire. To this homily (Heb. i.–xii.) is appended a concluding chapter (probably by the author himself) which transforms it into a letter. The author is a church-teacher of the second generation, as he frankly confesses himself (ii. 3); a disciple of Paul, to judge by his use of Paul's doctrine and some of his epistles, especially Romans. To judge by his rhetorical style and his Alexandrian ideas and mode of thought, he is the sort of teacher Apollos will have been. Just at present he is separated from his flock (xiii. 19). Where they are we can only infer from xiii. 24, which conveys salutations from those in the writer's neighbourhood who are "from Italy." He himself is probably among the Pauline churches, for he sends news of Timothy (xiii. 23) and hopes to come soon in company with him. Ephesus, where Apollos was at last accounts, may possibly be the place of writing. Hebrews would seem then to be written to Rome, long after the first "great fight of afflictions" (the Neronian outbreak of 64) and when the danger of "fainting under the chastening" of a second persecution (that of Domitian *c.* 90) was imminent. Such slight indications as we have of a literary relation between Hebrews and 1st Peter suggest the priority of Hebrews, but the date and occasion must be nearly the same.

"James" is also a homily exhorting to patient endurance, but there is nothing to suggest its having ever been sent anywhere as a letter, save the brief superscription written in imitation of 1st Pet. i. 1. "James . . . to the twelve tribes of the Dispersion." Imagine the mode of delivery! Nor is it called forth by any special emergency. There is an allusion to false doctrine. It is the heresy (!) of "justification by faith apart from works." But the writer is no more conscious of contradicting Paul than is Luke in describing Paul's apostleship and gospel. He merely impersonates the 'bishop of bishops' addressing Christendom at large, deprecating the loquacity of the "many teachers," and commending the 'wisdom' of a "good life" instead. There is protest against oppression. But it is only the oppression of the poor by the rich in the Christian brotherhood. He returns to this subject con amore. Evidently the church of his age is characterized by worldliness both of thought and conduct, among clergy and laity. But all colour of region or period is wanting. Take 1st Peter, substitute the head of the Jerusalem succession for the head of the Roman, remove the Pauline doctrine, the traces of Jesus and his gospel of sonship, remove the special references to local conditions and particular emergencies, leaving only moral generalities, and the result will be not unlike the Epistle of James. The author has heard something of Paulinism, has read Hebrews (Jas. ii. 21–25; v. 10), and imitated 1st Peter (Jas. i. 1, 18, 21; iv. 6 *f.*; v. 20). Strong arguments have even been advanced to prove that he was not a Christian at all. He probably was, if only from his literary connection with the above-named earlier writings, and the influence exerted by his own on Hermas (Rome, 120–140), and perhaps Clement (Rome, 95). But as for connection with the historic Jesus—"Elijah" is his example of the man of prayer (v. 13–18), and "Job" and "the prophets" his "example of suffering and patience" (v. 10 *f.*). Hebrews can show more of the influence of Jesus than this (Heb. v. 7 *f*, xii. 2–4). Like

Hermas (who, however, does not even mention the name of Jesus) 'James' thinks of Him simply as "the Lord of glory," without raising the question how He came to be such.

Apart from the superscription, whose object is only to clothe the homily with the authority of a name revered throughout the 'catholic' church, there is nothing to connect James with Syria rather than any other region outside Paul's mission-field. Even Palestine might be its place of origin if the date were late enough to account for the Greek style. At all events it comes first to our knowledge at Rome. There is some reason to think that Clement of Rome (A.D. 95), whose moralizing is of a similar type, has been directly influenced by James. If so we have in James, Clement and Hermas a series illustrative of the decline at Rome of the Pauline gospel of conscious revelation and inspiration toward the hum-drum levels of mere 'catholic' catechetics.

With every allowance for differences among critics as to date and origin of the non-controversial epistles of the sub-apostolic age, it is easy to see that the resistless march of events is taking up and accomplishing Paul's effort and prayer for the unity of the two branches of the Church. One great event of this period, which for us stands out with startling vividness upon the pages of history, is curiously without trace or reflection in this literature. We search the New Testament in vain for the slightest allusion (outside the writings directly or indirectly derived from Palestine itself) to the fall of Jerusalem in A.D. 70, and the consequent cessation of Jewish national life and temple ceremonial. The remoteness of the writers with whom we are dealing both in time and national interest from the affairs of Jerusalem is not the only cause. The fate of the temple had no effect to weaken the types of Judaism with which the church of the sub-apostolic age had to contend. The Pharisaic legalism of the synagogue became only the stronger when the hollow Sadducean priesthood collapsed, and temple ceremonial became simply a ceremonial on paper, the affair no longer of priest and Levite, but of scribe and Pharisee. So also with the denationalized Judaism of the Dispersion, a more insidious danger for early converts from heathenism than the stricter, legalistic type. The crushing of the nationalistic rebellion, the temporary suppression of the war-party, the Zealots, only strengthened and promoted Pharisaism, and the Dispersion was scarcely affected by the losses of the war. When Jerusalem and the temple fell, temple and city had become entirely superfluous factors to both parties in the great strife of church versus synagogue. Hebrews knows of a type of Judaism which is formidable by reason of the appeal of its ordinances of angels and its sacerdotal system written in a book of acknowledged divine authority. But the characteristic point is that in Hebrews, as truly as in Barnabas and Justin Martyr, it is only the prescription and not the practice which is in question. But for the fact that the "new testament" of Heb. ix. 15 is still unwritten, its controversy might properly be described as a battle of books.

On the other hand the pressure of persecution without, combined with the disappearance of creative leadership within, is visibly forcing the independent provinces of Christendom toward organic unity under the principle of apostolic authority. First Peter is the first and greatest evidence of this tendency to union promoted by external pressure. Hebrews and James follow as illustrative of the need felt for maintaining the standards both of doctrine and of morals at their full height. Christianity must not be thought of as on a level with Judaism, it is the final and universal revelation. It must not be practised half-heartedly, with "double-mindedness," nor in vain philosophizing and professions belied by deeds. It must be obeyed as a new and royal law, the mirror of divine perfection.

If, then, we turn from these evidences of general conditions in church and empire to the inward dangers revealed by the writings against heresy, we shall see how this disruptive influence, already distinctly apprehended in Paul's later writings, makes itself more and more strongly felt, and in more and more definite form, with Ephesus and the churches of Asia as its chief breeding-place.

The Pastoral Epistles in their present form cannot be dated much before the time when they begin to be used by Ignatius and Polycarp (110–117). Indeed some phrases (perhaps editorial additions) seem to imply a still later date, as when in 1st Tim. vi. 20, Timothy is warned against the " antitheses of miscalled Gnosis," as if with direct reference to Marcion's system of this title. Their avowed purpose is to counteract the inroads of heresy, and the remedy applied is ecclesiastical authority and discipline. Far more of Paul's inspired gospel of sonship and liberty, far more of his conception of the redemption in Christ as a triumph over the spiritual world-rulers of this darkness, is found in 1st Peter and Hebrews than here. Nothing appears of Paul's broad horizon, his spirit of missionary conquest, his devotion to the unity of Jew and Gentile in their common access to the Father in one Spirit. There is no trace of the great Pauline doctrines of the conflict of flesh and spirit, the superseding of the dispensation of Law by the dispensation of Grace, the Adoption, the Redemption, the Inheritance. The attention is turned wholly to local conditions, maintenance of the transmitted doctrine and order, resistance to the advance of " vain talk," " Jewish fables," " foolish questionings, genealogies and strifes about the Law," which go hand in hand with moral laxity. In short the outlook and temper are those of the Epistle of James, while the remedy is that of Acts and the Epistles of Ignatius. The Paul who here speaks is not the missionary and mystic, but the shrewd ecclesiastic. There is only too much evidence to show that in the Pauline mission-field the remedy resorted to against the licence in thought and action which threatened decadence and dissolution after apostolic inspiration had died out, was the religion of authority, doctrinal and disciplinary, not the religion of the Spirit. Ecclesiastical appointees take the place as teachers and defenders of the faith of those who had been the inspired apostles and prophets of its extension.

And on the other side are the false teachers. They are of Jewish character in their doctrine, aspiring to be " teachers of the Law " though really ignorant of its meaning. The worst of them are actual Jews (Tit. i. 10), which implies that some were not. Moreover the type of doctrine is still less like the Pharisaism of the synagogue than the " philosophy and vain deceit " rebuked by Paul at Colossæ. There is similar distinction of meats (treated in 2nd Tim. iv. 1–5 as a doctrine of " seducing spirits and demons "), and a prohibition of wine and marriage. There is side by side with this ascetic tendency one equally marked toward libertinism and love of money (2nd Tim. iii.

1–9). Both phases remind us of the "concision" of Paul's later letters. But besides the larger development new features appear of Hellenistic rather than Jewish type. The new doctrine of the resurrection as something "past already" is more closely connected with the Pauline mysticism, the present union of the believer with the life of Christ "hid in God," than with the Jewish idea of return to earth in resuscitated flesh. The Paulinist of the Pastorals is already foreshadowing the great conflict of Ignatius, Justin and Irenæus against those who "denied the resurrection," perverting (as the fathers allege) the meaning of Paul's saying, "flesh and blood cannot inherit the kingdom of God" (*cf.* 2nd Pet. iii. 16). And the Pastorals tend toward the un-Pauline doctrine soon to be formulated in the 'catholic' church: "I believe in the resurrection of the *flesh*." Again the false doctrine now distinctly avows itself a form of Gnosis. "They profess that they know God, but by their works they deny him, being abominable and disobedient, and unto every good work reprobate." And our Paulinist's remedy is the traditional doctrine, the "pattern of sound words," the "deposit" of the Church teacher, more especially the wholesome words, "even the words of our Lord Jesus Christ, and the doctrine which is according to godliness." Thus even the rich, if they do good, and become "rich in good works" will "lay up in store for themselves a good foundation against the time to come."

We have only to place these pseudo-Pauline writings side by side with the Epistles of John and Ignatius to recognize the advance of the heresy which soon declared itself as Gnostic Doketism, with the Jew Cerinthus at Ephesus as its principal exponent. Moreover this steadily increasing inward danger of the Paulne mission-field, a danger not merely sporadic like the outbursts of persecution, but constant and increasing, is forcing the two great branches of the Christian brotherhood together on the basis of 'catholicity' and the 'apostolic' tradition. Between the churches of the Ægean and that of Rome, where both parties stand on neutral ground, there are exchanged generous and sympathetic assurances of essential unity of doctrine in the great outbreak of persecution in 85–90. Among the Pauline churches themselves there is an irresistible reaction against the vagaries and moral laxity of heretical teaching toward 'apostolic' tradition and ecclesiastical authority. It appears with almost startling vividness in the Pastoral Epistles, and meets its answer from without, perhaps from Rome, perhaps from Syria, in the homily dressed as an encyclical called the Epistle of James. It is not hard to foresee what sort of Christian unity is destined to come about. Nevertheless the creative spirit and genius of Paul was to find expression in one more splendid product of Ephesus before the Roman unity was to be achieved.—But before we take up the writings of the great 'theologian' of Ephesus we must trace the growth in Syria and at Rome of the Literature of the Church Teacher and Prophet.

PART III

THE LITERATURE OF CATECHIST AND PROPHET

CHAPTER VI

THE MATTHÆAN TRADITION OF THE PRECEPTS OF JESUS

As we have seen in our study of the later literature addressed to, or emanating from, the Pauline mission-field, the church teacher and ecclesiastic who there took up the pen after the death of Paul had scarcely any alternative but to follow the literary model of the great founder of Gentile Christianity. Inevitably the typical literary product of this region became the apostolic letter, framed on the model of Paul's, borrowing his phraseology and ideas, when not actually embodying fragments from his pen and covering itself with his name. Homilies are made over into "epistles." Even 'prophecy,' to obtain literary circulation, must have prefixed epistles of "the Spirit" to the churches; and when at last a gospel is produced, this too is accompanied, as we shall see, by three successive layers of enclosing 'epistles.'

At the seat of 'apostolic' Christianity it was equally inevitable that the literary products should follow a different model. Here, from the beginning, the standard of authority had been the commandment of Jesus. Apostleship had meant ability to transmit his teaching, not endowment with insight into the mystery of the divine purpose revealed in his cross and resurrection. "The gospel" was the gospel *of* Jesus. The letters of Paul, if they circulated at all in Syria and Cilicia at this early time, have had comparatively small effect on writers like Luke and James. At Rome the case was somewhat different. Here Pauline influence had been effectually superimposed upon an originally Jewish-Christian stock. The Roman Gospel of Mark, accordingly, has just the characteristics we should expect from this Petro-Pauline community. Antioch, too, though at the disruption over the question of table-fellowship it took the side of James, Peter, and Barnabas against Paul, had always had a strong Gentile element. But Jerusalem, the church of the apostles and elders, with its caliphate in the family of Jesus, and its zeal for Jewish institutions and the Law, was the pre-eminent seat of traditional authority. No other gospel, oral or written, could for a moment compare in its eyes with its own cherished treasury of the precepts of Jesus. Its own estimate of itself as conservator of orthodoxy, and custodian of the sacred deposit, vividly reflected from the pages of Hegesippus, was increasingly accepted by the other churches. 'James' and 'Jude' were probably not the real names of the writers of these 'general' or 'catholic' epistles; but they show in what direction men looked when there was need to counteract a widespread tendency to moral relaxation and vain disputations, or to demoralizing heresy.

We have also seen how inevitable was the reaction after Paul's death, even among his own churches, toward a historic standard of authority. Even more marked than the disposition to draw together in fraternal sympathy under persecution, is the reliance shown by the Pastoral Epistles on "health-giving words, even the words of our Lord Jesus Christ" (1st Tim. vi. 3), and on a consolidated apostolic succession as a bulwark against the disintegrating advance of heresy. In (proconsular) Asia early in the second century there is an unmistakable and sweeping disposition to "turn to the word handed down to us from the beginning" (*Ep. of Polyc.*, vii.) against those who were "perverting the sayings of the Lord to their own lusts." The ancient "word of prophecy" and the former revelations granted to apostolic seers were also turned to account by men like Papias and the author of 2nd Peter against those who "denied the resurrection and judgment."

This Papias of Hierapolis, the friend and colleague of Polycarp, had undertaken in opposition to " the false teachers, and those who have so very much to say," to write (probably after the utter destruction of the community of 'apostles, elders, and witnesses' at Jerusalem in 135), *an Exposition of the Sayings of the Lord.* He based the work on authentic tradition of the Jerusalem witnesses, two of whom (Aristion, and John 'the Elder') were still living at the time of his inquiries. In fact, this much debated " John the Elder," clearly distinguished by Papias from John the " disciple of the Lord," may be identified, in our judgment, with the John mentioned by Eusebius and Epiphanius midway in the succession of 'Elders' of the Jerusalem church between A.D. 62 and 135. Epiphanius dates his death in 117. Papias gives us practically all the information we have regarding the beginnings of gospel literature. He may have known all four of our Gospels. He certainly knew Revelation and " vouched for its trustworthiness," doubtless against the deniers of the resurrection and judgment. He " used testimonies " from 1st John, and probably the saying of Jesus of John xiv. 2; but he seems to have based his *Exposition* on two gospels only, giving what he had been able to learn of their history from travellers who reported to him testimonies of 'the elders.' Papias' two gospels were our Matthew and our Mark, whose differences he reconciled by what the Jerusalem elders had reported as to their origin. Matthew, according to these authorities (?), represented in its Greek form a collection of the Precepts of the Lord which had formerly been current in the original Aramaic, so that its circulation had of course been limited to Palestine. The original compiler had been the Apostle Matthew. Various Greek equivalents of this compilation had taken its place where Aramaic was not current. Thus Papias, in explicit dependence on "the Elder" so far as Mark is concerned, but without special designation of his authority for the statement regarding Matthew. It is even possible that his representation that the primitive Matthew was "in the Hebrew tongue" may be due to rumours whose real starting-point was nothing more than the *Gospel of the Nazarenes*, a product of *c.* 110–140 which misled many later fathers, particularly Jerome. We cannot afford, however, to slight the general bearing of testimony borne by one such as Papias regarding the origins of gospel composition, and particularly the two branches into which the tradition was divided. For Papias had made diligent inquiry. Moreover his witness does not stand alone, but has the support of still more ancient reference (*e. g.* 1st Tim. vi. 3, Acts i. 1) and the internal evidence of the Synoptic Gospels themselves. The motive for his statement is apologetic. Differences between the two Gospels had been pointed out on the score both of words and events. Papias shows that Gospel tradition is not to be held responsible for verbal agreement between the two parallel reports of the Lord's words. The differences are attributable to translation. So, too, regarding events. Exact correspondence of Mark with Matthew (or other gospels) is not to be looked for, especially as regards the order; because Mark had not himself been a disciple, and could not get the true order from Peter, whose anecdotes he reproduced; for when Mark wrote Peter was no longer living. Mark has reproduced faithfully and accurately his recollection of "things either said or done," as related by Peter. But Peter had had no such intention as Matthew of making a systematic compilation (*syntagma*) of the sayings of the Lord, and had only related his anecdotes "as occasion required." If the tradition regarding Matthew, as well as that regarding Mark, was derived from the Elder, he, too, as well as Papias, knew the Greek Matthew; regarding it as a "translation" of the apostolic *Logia*, he naturally makes Matthew the standard and accounts as above for the wide divergence of Mark as to order.

The Jerusalem elder who thus differentiates the two great branches of gospel tradition into Matthæan Precepts and Petrine Sayings and Doings, is probably "the Elder John"; for this elder's "traditions" were so copiously cited by Papias as to lead Irenæus, and after him Eusebius, to the unwarranted inference of personal contact. Irenæus even identified the Elder John with the Apostle, thus transporting not only him, but the entire body of "Elders and disciples" from Jerusalem to Asia, a pregnant misapprehension to which we must return later. In the meantime we must note that this fundamental distinction between *syntagmas* of the Precepts, and narratives of the Sayings and Doings, carries us back as far as it is possible to penetrate into the history of gospel composition. The primitive work of the Apostle Matthew, was probably done in and for Jerusalem and vicinity—certainly so if written in Aramaic. The date, if early tradition may be believed, was "when Peter and Paul were preaching and founding the church at Rome." Oral tradition must have begun the process even earlier.[1] Mark's work was done at Rome, according to internal evidence no less than by the unanimous voice of early tradition. It dates from "after the death of Peter" (64–5) according to ancient tradition. According to the internal evidence it was written certainly not long before, and probably some few years after, the overthrow of Jerusalem and the temple (70). At the time of Papias' writing, then (*c.* 145), all four gospels were probably known, though only Matthew and Mark were taken as authoritative because (indirectly) apostolic. At the time of prosecution of his

[1] Some authorities of the first rank think there is evidence of literary dependence in 1st Cor. i. 18–21 on the Saying (Matt. xi. 25–27 = Lk. x. 21 *f.*).

inquiries the voice of (Palestinian) tradition was still "living and abiding." If, as tenses and phraseology seem to imply, this means Aristion and the Elder John (*ob.* 117 ?) it is reasonable to regard it as extending back over a full generation. The original Matthew was even then (*c.* 100), and in Palestine itself, a superseded book. It had three successors, if not more, two Greek and one Aramaic, all still retaining their claim to the name and authority of Matthew [1]; but all had been recast in a narrative frame, which at least in the case of our canonical first Gospel was borrowed from the Roman work of Mark. So far as the remaining fragments of its rivals enable us to judge, the same is true in their case also, though to a less extent. It is quite unmistakably true of Luke, the gospel of Antioch, that its narrative represents the same "memorabilia of Peter"; for so Mark's gospel came to be called. Thus the Petrine story appears almost from the start to have gained undisputed supremacy. But side by side with this remarkable fact as to gospel *narrative* is the equally notable confirmation of the other statements of 'the Elders' regarding the Precepts. For all modern

[1] The orthodox Aramaic *Gospel of the Nazarenes* borrows from Luke as well as Matthew, but speaks in the name of "Matthew." This apostle was also regarded as author of the *Gospel according to the Hebrews*, a heretical product of *c.* 120, current in Greek among the Jewish Christians of Palestine (Ebionites).

criticism admits, that besides the material of Mark, which both Matthew and Luke freely incorporate, omitting very little, our first and third evangelists have embodied, in (usually) the same Greek translation but in greatly varied order, large sections from one or more early compilations of the Sayings of Jesus.

It is indispensable to a historical appreciation of the environment out of which any gospel has arisen that we realize that no community ever produced and permanently adopted as its " gospel " a *partial* presentation of the message of salvation. To its mind the writing must have embodied, for the time at least, the message, the whole message, and nothing but the message. Change of mind as to the essential contents of the message would involve supplementation or alteration of the written gospel employed. No writing of the kind would be produced with tacit reference to some other for another aspect of the truth.

It was not, then, the mere limitation of its language which caused the ancient Matthæan Sayings (the so-called *Logia*) to be superseded and disappear; nor is mere " translation " the word to describe that which took its place. The growth of Christianity in the Greek-speaking world not only called upon Jerusalem to pour out its treasure of evangelic tradition in the language of the empire, but stimulated a sense of its own increasing need. That which could once be supplied by eye-witnesses, the testimony of Jesus' mighty works, his death and resurrection, was now fast disappearing. And simultaneously the appreciation of its importance was growing. It was impossible to be blind to the conquests made by the gospel *about* Jesus. Enclosed in it, as part of its substance the gospel *of* Jesus found its final resting-place, much as the mother church itself was later taken up and incorporated in a catholic Christendom. So it is that in the Elder's time the church of the 'apostles, elders and witnesses' have done more than merely supersede their Aramaic (?) *Syntagma* of the Precepts by "translations." They had adopted alongside of it from Rome Mark's "Memorabilia of Peter" as to "things either said or done by the Lord." We can see indeed from the apologetic way in which 'the Elder' speaks of Mark's limitations (Peter is not to be held responsible for the lack of order) that Mark's authority is still held quite secondary to Matthew's; but the very fact that his work is given authoritative standing at all, still more the fact that it has become the framework into which the old-time *syntagma* has been set, marks a great and fundamental change of view as to what constitutes "the gospel."

No mere *syntagma* of the Precepts of Jesus has ever come down to us, though the papyrus leaves of "Sayings of Jesus" discovered in 1897 at Behneseh in Egypt by Grenfell and

Hunt had something of this character.[1] It was impossible that any community outside the most primitive one, where personal "witnesses of the Lord" still survived "until the times of Trajan," could be satisfied with a "gospel" which gave only the precepts of Jesus without so much as an account of his crucifixion and resurrection. And, strange as it may seem, the evidence of Q (*i. e.* the coincident material in Matthew and Luke not derived from Mark), as judged by nearly all critics, is that no narrative of the kind was given in the early compilation of discourses from which this element was mainly derived. After the "witnesses," apostolic and other, had begun to disappear, a mere *syntagma* of Jesus' sayings could not suffice. It became inevitable that the precepts should be embodied in the story. And yet we have at least two significant facts to corroborate the intimations of ancient tradition that this combination was long postponed. (1) When it is at last effected, and certainly in the regions of southern Syria,[2] there is even there practically

[1] It was superscribed "These are the . . . words (*logoi* as in the Pastoral Epistles, not *logia* as in Papias and Polycarp) which Jesus the living Lord spoke to the disciples and Thomas."

[2] The possibility should be left open that the Greek Matthew was written in Egypt (cf. Matt. ii. 15), as some critics hold. From the point of view of the church historian, however, Egypt must really be classed as in "the regions of southern Syria." Its relations with Jerusalem were close and constant."

nothing left of authentic *narrative* material but the Petrine tradition as compiled by Mark at Rome. Our Matthew, a Palestinian Jew, the only writer of the New Testament who consistently uses the Hebrew Bible, makes a theoretical reconstruction of the order of events in the Galilean ministry, but otherwise he just incorporates Mark substantially as it was. What he adds in the way of narrative is so meagre in amount, and so manifestly inferior and apocryphal in character, as to prove the extreme poverty of his resources of oral tradition of this type. Luke has somewhat larger, and (as *literary* products) better, narrative additions than Matthew's; but the amount is still extremely meagre, and often *historically* of slight value. Some of it reappears in the surviving fragments of the *Preaching of Peter*. To sum up, there is outside of Mark *no* considerable amount of historical material, canonical or uncanonical, for the story of Jesus. This fact would be hard to account for if in the regions where witnesses survived, the first generation really took an interest in perpetuating narrative tradition. (2) The *order* of even such events as secured perpetuation was already hopelessly lost at a time more remote than the writing of our earliest gospel. This is true not only for Mark, as 'the Elder' frankly confesses, but for Matthew, Luke and every one else. Unchronological as Mark's order often is (and the tradition as to the 'casual anecdotes' agrees with the critical phenomena of the text), it is vastly more historical than Matthew's reconstruction. On the other hand Luke, while expressly undertaking to improve in this special respect upon his predecessors, almost never ventures to depart from the order of Mark, and when he does has never the support of Matthew, and usually not that of real probability. In short, incorrect as they knew the order of Mark to be, it was the best that could be had in the days when evangelists began to go beyond the mere *syntagmas*, and to write "gospels" as we understand them, or, in their own language, "the things which Jesus began *both* to do *and* to teach" (Acts i. 1). From these two great outstanding phenomena of gospel criticism alone it would be apparent that the distinction dimly perceived in the tradition of the Jerusalem elders reported by Papias, and indeed by many later writers, is no illusion, but an important and vital fact.

A third big, unexpected fact looms up as we round the capes of critical analysis, subtracting from Matthew and Luke first the elements peculiar to each, then that derived by each from Mark. It is a fact susceptible, however, of various interpretation. To some it only proves either the futility of criticism, or the worthlessness of ancient tradition. To us it proves simply that the process of transition in Palestine, the home of evangelic tradition, from the primitive *syntagma* of

Precepts, framed on the plan of the Talmudic treatise known as *Pirke Aboth*, or "Sayings of the Fathers," to the Greek type of narrative gospel, was a longer and more complex one than has commonly been imagined. A cursory statement of the results of critical efforts to reproduce the so-called "second source" of Matthew and Luke (Mark being considered the first), will serve to bring out the fact to which we refer, and at the same time, we hope, to throw light upon the history of gospel development.

The mere process of subtraction above described to obtain the element Q offers no serious difficulties, and for those who attach value to the tradition of 'the Elders' it is natural to anticipate that the remainder will show traits corresponding to the description of an apostolic *syntagma* of sayings of the Lord translated from the Aramaic, in short the much-desired *Logia* of Matthew. The actual result is disappointing to such an expectation. The widely, though perhaps somewhat thoughtlessly accepted equivalence Q = the *Logia* is simply false. Q is *not* the *Logia*. It is not a *syntagma*, nor even a consistent whole, and as it lay before our first and third evangelists it was not (for a considerable part at least) in Aramaic. True, Q does consist *almost* exclusively of discourse material, a large part of which has only topical order, and is wholly, or mainly, destitute of narrative connection. Also we find traces here and there of translation at some period from the Aramaic, though not more in the Q element than in Mark. But to those who looked for immediate confirmation of the tradition the result has been on the whole disappointing. Some, more particularly among English critics, have considered it to justify a falling back upon the vaguer generalities of the once prevalent theory of oral tradition. In reality we are simply called upon to renew the process of discrimination. Most of the Q material has the saying-character and is strung together with that lack of all save topical order which we look for in a *syntagma*. But parts of it, such as the Healing of the Centurion's servant (Matt. viii. 5–10, 13=Luke vii. 1–10), or the Preaching of the Baptist and Temptation Story (Matt. iii. 7–10, 12; iv. 2–11=Luke iii. 7–9, 17; iv. 2–13), obstinately refuse to be brought under this category. Moreover, the latter section has the unmistakable motive of presenting Jesus *in his character and ministry* as "the Son of God," precisely as in Mark. It begins by introducing Jesus on the stage at the baptism of John, after the ancient narrative outline (Acts i. 22; x. 37 *f.*), and cannot be imagined as forming part of anything else but a *narrative* having the conclusion characteristic of our own type of gospel. Other considerable sections of Q, such as the Question of John's Disciples and Discourse of Jesus on those that were 'Stumbled' in him (Matt. xi. 2–11, 16–27; Luke vii. 18–35; x.

13–22), share with the Baptism and Temptation section not only the doctrinal motive of commending Jesus in his person and ministry as the longed-for Son of God, but in a number of characteristics which set them quite apart from the general mass of precepts and parables in Q. We can here mention only the following: (1) the coincidence in language between Matthew and Luke is much greater in these sections of Q, often even greater than in the sections borrowed from Mark, showing clearly the existence of a common document written not in Aramaic, but in the Greek language. (2) This material, unlike most of Q, has served as a source and model in many portions of Mark. (3) It is for the most part not included in the five great blocks into which Matthew has divided the Precepts by means of a special concluding formula (vii. 28; xi. 1; xiii. 53; xix. 1, and xxvi. 1) but appears outside, in the form of supplements to the Markan narrative (iii. 7—iv. 11; viii. 5–13, 18–22, xi. 2–27; xii. 38–45, etc.). Finally (4) the Q material of this type seems to be given more copiously by Luke than by Matthew, and with something more than mere conjecture of his own as to its historical occasion. In fact, since it appears that at least this element of Q was known to Mark, there is nothing to justify exclusion from it of such material as the Transfiguration story, though in this case it would be needful to prove that Mark was not the source. Similarly it would be reasonable to think of Luke's wide divergence from Mark in his story of the Passion as occasioned by his preference for material derived from this source. Only, since Matthew has preferred to follow Mark, we have no means of determining whence Luke did derive his new and here often valuable material.

The existence, then, of an element of Q which quite fails to correspond to what we take the Matthæan *syntagma* to have been by no means proves either the futility of criticism or the worthlessness of the ancient tradition. It only shows that our synoptic evangelists were not the first to attempt the combination of discourse with narrative, but that Luke at least had a predecessor in the field, to whom all are more or less indebted. Criticism and tradition together show that there are two great streams from which all historically trustworthy material has been derived. The one is Evangelic Story, and is mainly derived from Mark's outline of the ministry based on the anecdotes of Peter, though some elements come from another source, principally preserved by Luke, which we must discuss in a later chapter devoted to the growth of Petrine story at Rome and Antioch. The other stream, "Words of the Lord," comes from Jerusalem, and is always associated in all its forms with the name of Matthew. We have every reason for accepting the statement that as early as the founding of the church in Rome (45–50) the Apostle Matthew had begun the work of compiling the Precepts of Jesus, in a form serviceable to the object of "teaching men to observe all things whatsoever he had commanded." Our present Gospel of Matthew, however, is neither this work nor a translation of it; for the only three things told us about the apostle's work are all irreconcilable with the characteristics of our Matthew. The compilation of "Words of the Lord" was (1) a *syntagma* and not, like Mark, an outline of the ministry. It was (2) written in Aramaic; whereas our Matthew is an original Greek composition. It was (3) by an apostle who had personal acquaintance with Jesus; whereas our first evangelist is to the last degree dependent upon the confessedly defective story of Mark. Still if we take our Matthew as the last link in the long chain of development, covering perhaps half a century, and including such by-products as the *Gospel according to the Hebrews* and the *Gospel of the Nazarenes*, we may obtain a welcome light upon the environment out of which has come down the work which an able scholar justly declared, "the most important book ever written, the Gospel according to Matthew."

The language in which it was written was alone sufficient to place the Greek Matthew beyond all possible competition in the larger world from Aramaic rivals. But its comprehensiveness and catholicity still further helped it to the position which it soon attained as the most widely used of all the gospels. Matthew is not only in its whole structure a composite gospel, but shows in high degree the catholicizing tendency of the times. Just as it frankly adopts the Roman-Petrine narrative of Mark with slightest possible modification, so also it places in Peter's hand with equal frankness the primacy in apostolic succession. Almost the only additions it makes to Mark's account of the public ministry are the story of Peter's walking on the sea (xiv. 28–33), and his payment of the temple tribute for Christ and himself with the coin from the fish's mouth (xvii. 24–27). The latter story introduces the chapter on the exercise of rulership in "the church" (ch. xviii.), beginning with the disciples' question : "Who *then* is greatest in the kingdom ?" Peter is again in it the one salient figure (xviii. 21). An equally important addition, connected with xviii. 17 *f.* is the famous committal to Peter of the power of the keys, with the declaration making him for his confession the 'Rock' foundation of "the church." This addition to Mark's story of the rebuke of Peter at Cæsarea Philippi, is one which decidedly alters its bearing, and seems even to borrow the very language of Gal. i. 16 *f.* in order to exalt the apostleship of Peter. In fact, the Roman gospel and the Palestinian almost reverse the rôles we should expect Peter to play in each. Matthew alone makes Peter "the first" (x. 2), while Mark seems to take special pains to record rebukes of the twelve and the brethren of the Lord, and especially the rebukes called down upon themselves by Peter, or Peter and John.

In respect to the primacy of Peter we can observe a certain difference even among the Palestinian gospels which succeeded to the primitive *syntagma* of Matthew. Little, indeed, is known of the orthodox *Gospel of the Nazarenes*, beyond its relatively late and composite character; for it borrowed from Matthew, Mark and Luke in turn. Its list of apostles, however, begins with "John and James the sons of Zebedee," *then* "Simon and Andrew," and winds up: "Thee also, Matthew, did I call, as thou wert sitting at the seat of custom, and thou followedst me." The anti-Pauline *Gospel according to the Hebrews* shows its conception of the seat of apostolic authority by giving to "James the Just" the place of Peter as recipient of that first manifestation of the risen Lord, which laid the foundation of the faith. Why then does the Greek Palestinian gospel, in contrast with its rivals, lay such special stress on the primacy of Peter?

From the cautious and (as it were) deprecatory tone of the appendix to John (John xxi.) in seeking to commend the "other disciple whom Jesus loved" as worthy to be accepted as a "true witness" without detriment to the acknowledged authority of Peter as chief under-shepherd of the flock, we may infer that not at Rome alone, but wherever there was question of 'apostolic' tradition, the authority of Peter was coming rapidly to the fore. The tendency at Antioch is even more marked than at Rome, as is manifest from Acts. If, then, it seems stronger still in a region where we should expect the authority of James to be put forward, this need not be taken as a specifically Roman trait. We must realize the sharp antagonism which existed in Palestine from the time of the Apostolic council down, between (1) the consistent legalists, who maintained down to the period of Justin (153) and the *Clementine Homilies and Recognitions* (180–200), their bitter hostility to Paul and his gospel of Gentile freedom from the Law; and (2) the 'catholic,' or liberal, Jewish-Christians, who took the standpoint of the Pillars. It is but one of many indications of its 'catholic' tendency that our Matthew increases the emphasis on the apostolic authority of Peter to the point of an actual primacy. The phenomenon must be judged in the light of the disappearance or suppression of all evangelic story save what came under the name of Peter, and the tendency in Acts to bring under his name even the entire apostleship to the Gentiles. Peter is not yet in these early writings the representative of Rome, but of *catholicity*. The issue in Matthew is not as between Rome and some other dominant see, but (as the reflection of the language of Gal. i. 17 *f.* in Matt. xvi. 17 shows) as between 'catholic' apostolic authority and the unsafe tendencies of Pauline independence.

Nevertheless, for all his leanings to catholicity the Greek Matthew has not wholly succeeded in excluding materials which still reflect Jewish-Christian hostility to Paul, or at least to the tendencies of Pauline Christianity. Over and over again special additions are made in Matthew to emphasize a warning against the workers of "lawlessness." The exhortation of Jesus in Luke vi. 42–45 to effect (self-)reformation not on the surface, nor in word, but by change of the inward root of disposition fructifying in deeds, is altered in Matt. vii. 15–22 into a warning against the "false prophets" who work "lawlessness," and who must be judged by their fruits. They make the confession of Lordship (*cf.* Rom. x. 9), but are not obedient to Jesus' commandment, and lack good works. In particular the test of Mark ix. 38–40 is directly reversed. The principle "Whosoever is not against us is for us" is not to be trusted. A teacher may exercise the 'spiritual gifts' of prophecy, exorcism, and miracles wrought in the name of Jesus, and still be a reprobate. A similar (and most incongruous) addition is made to Mark's parable of the Patient Husbandman (Mark iv. 26–29), in Matt. xiii. 24–30, and reiterated in a specially appended "interpretation" (xiii. 36–43). This addition likens the "workers of lawlessness" to tares sown alongside the good seed of the word by "an enemy." A similar incongruous attachment is made to the parable of the Marriage feast (Matt. xxii. 1–14; *cf.* Luke xiv. 15–24) to warn against the lack of the 'garment of good works.' Finally, Matthew closes his whole series of the discourses of Jesus with a group of three parables developed with great elaboration and rhetorical effect, out of relatively slight suggestions as found elsewhere. The sole theme of the series is the indispensableness of good works in the judgment (Matt. 25; *cf.* Luke xii. 35–38; xix. 11–28, and Mark ix. 37, 41). A similar interest appears in Matthew's insistence on the permanent obligation of the Law (v. (16) 17–20; xix. 16–22—in contrast with Mark x. 17–22), on respect for the temple (xvii. 24–27) and on the Davidic descent of Jesus, with fulfilment of messianic promise in him (chh. i.–ii.; ix. 27). He limits the activity of Jesus to the Holy Land (xv. 22; contrast Mark vii. 24 *f.*), makes him in sending forth the Twelve (x. 5 *f.*) specifically forbid mission work among Samaritans or Gentiles, and while the prohibition is finally removed in xxviii. 18–20, the apostolic seat cannot be removed, but remains as in x. 23, among "the cities of Israel" to the end of the world.

There is probably no more of intentional opposition to Paul or to his gospel in all this than in James or Luke. We cannot for example regard it as more than accidental coincidence that in the phrase "an enemy hath done this," in the parable of the tares, we have the same epithet which the Ebionite literature applies to Paul. But enough remains to indicate how strongly Jewish-Christian prejudices and limitations still affected our evangelist. With respect to date, the atmosphere is in all respects such as characterizes the period of the nineties.

It does not belong to our present purpose to analyze this gospel into its constituent elements. The process can be followed in many treatises on gospel criticism, and the results will be found summarized in *Introductions* to the New Testament such as the recent scholarly work of Moffatt. We have here but to note the general character and structure of the book as revealing the main outlines of its history and the conditions which gave it birth.

Matthew and Luke are alike in that both represent comparatively late attempts to combine the ancient Matthæan *syntagma* with the 'Memorabilia of Peter' compiled by Mark. But there is a great difference. Luke contemplates his work with some of the motives of the historian. He adopts the method of narrative, and therefore subordinates his discourse material to a conception (often confused enough) of sequence in space and time. Matthew, as the structure of his gospel, no less than his own avowal shows, had an aim more nearly corresponding to the ancient Palestinian type. The demand for the narrative form had become irresistible. It controlled even his later Greek and Aramaic rivals. But Matthew has subordinated the historical to the ethical motive. He aims at, and has rendered, just the service which his age demanded and for which it could look to no other region than Jerusalem, a full compilation of the commandments and precepts of Jesus.

The narrative framework is adopted from Mark without serious alteration, because this work had already proved its effectiveness in convincing men everywhere that Jesus was "the Christ, the Son of God." Like Luke, Matthew prefixes an account of Jesus' miraculous birth and childhood, because in his time (*c.* 90) the ancient "beginning of the gospel" with the baptism by John had given opportunity to the heresy of the Adoptionists, represented by Cerinthus, who maintained that Jesus *became* the Son of God at his baptism, a merely temporary "receptacle" of the Spirit. The prefixed chapters have no incarnation doctrine, and no doctrine of preexistence. They do not intend in their story of the miraculous birth to relate the incoming of a super-human or non-human being into the world, else they could not take up the pedigree of Joseph as exhibiting Jesus' title to the throne of David. Miracle attends and signalizes the birth of that "Son of David" who is destined to become the Son of God.

Apart from the mere question of attendant prodigy the aim of Matthew's story of the Infancy is such as should command the respect and sympathy of every rational thinker. Against all Doketic dualism it maintains that the Son of God is such from birth to death. The presence of God's Spirit with him is not a mere counterpart to demonic "possession," but is part of his nature as true man from the beginning.

But the doctrinal interest of Matthew scarcely goes beyond the point of proving that Jesus is the Christ foretold by the prophets. Doctrine as well as history is subordinate to the one great aim of teaching men to "observe all things whatsoever Jesus commanded."

CHAPTER VII

THE PETRINE TRADITION. EVANGELIC STORY

Of the extent to which the early church could do without narrative of Jesus' earthly ministry we have extraordinary evidences in the literature of Pauline Christianity on the one side and of Jewish Christianity on the other. For Paul himself, as we know, the real story of Jesus was a transcendental drama of the Incarnation, Redemption, and Exaltation. It is probable that when at last "three years" after his conversion he went up to Jerusalem "to get acquainted with Peter," the story he was interested to hear had even then more to do with that common apostolic witness of the resurrection appearances reproduced in 1st Cor. xv. 3–11, than with the sayings and doings of the ministry. As to this Paul preserves, as we have seen, an almost unbroken silence. And that which did not interest Paul, naturally did not interest his churches.

On the other hand those who could have perpetuated a full and authentic account of the ministry were almost incredibly slow to undertake the task; partly, no doubt, because of their vivid expectation of the immediate end of the world, but largely also because to their mind the data most in need of preservation were the 'life-giving words.' The impression of Jesus' character, his person and authority was not, as they regarded it, a thing to be gained from the historical outline of his career. It was established by the fact of the Resurrection, by the predictions of the prophets, which found fulfilment in the circumstances of Jesus' birth, particular incidents here and there in his career and fate, but most of all in his resurrection and the gifts of the Spirit which argued his present session at the right hand of God. Once this authority of Jesus was established the believer had only to observe his commandments as handed down by the apostles, elders and witnesses.

On all sides there was an indifference to such historical inquiry as the modern man would think natural and inevitable, an indifference that must remain altogether inexplicable to us unless we realize that until at least the time of the fourth evangelist the main proofs of messiahship were not looked for in Jesus' earthly career. His Christhood was thought of as something in the future, not yet realized. Even his resurrection and manifestation in glory "at the right hand of God," which is to both Paul (Rom. i. 4) and his predecessors (Acts ii. 32–36) the assurance that "God hath made him both Lord and Christ," is not yet the beginning of his specific messianic programme. Potentially this has begun, because Jesus has already been seated on the 'throne of glory,' "from henceforth expecting until his enemies be made the footstool of his feet." Practically it is not yet. The Christ is still a Christ that is to be. His messianic rule is delayed until the subjugation of the "enemies"; and this subjugation in turn is delayed by "the longsuffering of God, who willeth not that any should perish, but that all men should come to repentance." Meantime a special "outpouring of the Spirit" is given in 'tongues,' 'prophecies,' 'miracle working,' and the like, in fulfilment of scriptural promise, as a kind of coronation largess to all loyal subjects. This outpouring of the Spirit, then, is the great proof and assurance that the Heir has really ascended the 'throne of glory' in spite of the continuance of "all things as they were from the foundation of the world." These 'gifts' are "firstfruits of the Spirit," pledges of the ultimate inheritance, proofs both to believers and unbelievers of the complete Inheritance soon to be received. But the gifts have also a practical aspect. They are all endowments for *service*. The Great Repentance in Israel and among the Gentiles is not to be brought about without the cooperation of believers. The question which at once arises when the manifestation of the risen Christ is granted, "Lord, dost thou at this time restore the kingdom to Israel?" is therefore answered by the assurance that the time is in God's hand alone, but that the 'gifts of the Spirit,' soon to be imparted, are intended to enable believers to do their part, at home and abroad, toward effecting the Great Repentance (Acts i. 6–8).[1]

For a church which felt itself endowed with living and present evidences of the messianic power of Jesus it was naturally only a second thought (and not a very early one at that) to look back for proof to occurrences in Jesus' life in Galilee, however notable his career as "a prophet mighty in deed and word before God and all the people." The *present* gifts of his power would be (at least in demonstrative effect) "greater works than these." With those who had the resurrection testimony

[1] The parallel in Mark xvi. 14–18 is very instructive, but needs the recently discovered connection between verses 14 and 15 to complete the sense: "And they excused themselves (for their unbelief) saying, This age of lawlessness and unbelief is under the dominion of Satan, who by means of the unclean spirits prevents the truth and power of God from being apprehended. On this account reveal thy righteousness (*i. e.* justice, in the sense of Isa. lvi, 1 *b*) even now. And Christ replied to them, The limit of years of Satan's power is (already) fulfilled, but other terrible things are at hand; moreover I was delivered up to death on behalf of sinners in order that they might return unto the truth and sin no more, that they might inherit the spiritual and incorruptible glory which is in heaven." Then follows the mission into all the world and endowment with the gifts.

of 1st Cor. xv. 3–11, and even the recurrent experience of "visions and revelations of the Lord," anticipatory revelations of his messiahship, utterances, like that to Peter at Cæsarea Philippi, wherein Jesus only predicted the great work to be divinely accomplished through him, whether by life or death, in going up to Jerusalem, intimations which had been disregarded or disbelieved at the time, could not rank with present knowledge, experience and insight. They would be recalled merely as confirmatory foregleams of "the true light that now shineth," as the two who had received the manifestation at Emmaus exclaim, "Did not our heart burn within us while he talked to us in the way?"

We could not indeed psychologically account for the development of the resurrection faith after the crucifixion, if before it Jesus' life and utterances had not been such as to make his manifestation in glory seem to the disciples just what they *ought* to have expected. But, conversely, nothing is more certain than the fact that they *did not* expect it; and that when the belief had become established by other means, the attitude toward the "sayings and doings" maintained by those who had them to relate—as we know, the most successful missionary of all felt it no handicap to be entirely without them—was one of looking back into an obscure past for things whose pregnant significance became appreciable only in the light of present knowledge. "These things understood not his disciples at the first, but when Jesus was glorified, then remembered they that these things had been written of him, and that they had done these things unto him."

We are fortunate in having even one example of the "consecutive narratives" (*diegeses*) referred to in Luke i. 1. Our Mark is a gospel written purely and simply from this point of view, aiming only to show how the earthly career of Jesus gave evidence that this was the Son of God, predestined to exaltation to the right hand of power, with little attempt, if any, to bring in the precepts of the New Law. We should realize, however, that this is already a beginning in the process soon to become controlling, a process of carrying back into the earthly life of Jesus in Galilee of first this trait, then that, then all the attributes of the glorified Lord.

Ancient and reliable tradition informs us that this first endeavour to tell the story of "Jesus Christ the Son of God" was composed at Rome by John Mark, a former companion of both Peter and Paul, from data drawn from the anecdotes casually employed by Peter in his preaching. There is much to confirm this in the structure, the style, and the doctrinal object and standpoint of the Gospel.

To begin with, the date of composition cannot be far from 75. Mark is not only presupposed by both Matthew and Luke, but in their time had already acquired an extraordinary predominance. To judge by what remains to us of similar products, Mark in its own field might almost be said to reign supreme and reign alone. Such almost exclusive supremacy could not have been attained, even by a writing commonly understood to represent the preaching of Peter, short of a decade or more of years. On the other hand we have the reluctant testimony of antiquity, anxious to claim as much as possible of apostolic authority for the record, but unwilling to commit Peter to apparent contradictions of Matthew, that it was written after Peter's death (64–5).[1] Internal evidence would in fact bring down the date of the work in its present form a full decade thereafter. It is true that there are many structural evidences of more than one form of the narrative, and that the apocalyptic chapter (ch. xiii.), which furnishes most of the evidence of date, may well belong among the later supplements. But in the judgment of most critics this 'eschatological discourse' (almost the only connected discourse of the Gospel) is clearly framed in real retrospect upon the overthrow of Jerusalem and the temple, and the attendant tribulation on "those that are in Judæa." The writer applies a general saying of Jesus known to us from other sources about destroying and rebuilding the

[1] So Irenaeus (186) and (by implication) Papias. Clement of Alexandria (210) meets the difficulty by alleging that Peter was still alive, but gave no aid to the writer.

temple specifically to the demolition effected by Titus (70). He warns his readers in the same connection that "the end" is not to follow immediately upon the great Judæan war, but only when the powers of evil in the heavenly places, powers inhabiting sun, moon and stars, are shaken (xiii. 21–27). The Pauline doctrine of 2nd Thess. ii. 1–12 is adopted, but with careful avoidance of the prediction that the "man of sin" is to appear "in the temple of God." Paul's "man of sin" is now identified with Daniel's "abomination that maketh desolate" (Dan. xii. 11), which therefore is spoken of as "he" (masculine). "His" appearance will prelude the great Judæan tribulation; but his standing place is ill-defined. It is only "where he ought not." Matthew (following his usual practice) returns more nearly to the language of Daniel. With him the "Abomination" is again an object standing "in *a* holy place." But Matthew is already applying the prophecy to another tribulation still to come. He does not see that Mark refers to the sack of Jerusalem on which he himself looks back in his addition to the parable of the Supper (Matt. xxii. 6 *f.*; *cf.* Luke xiv. 15–24), but takes Mark xiii. 14–23 as Jesus' prediction of a great final tribulation *still to come.*

Mark's crudities of language and style, his frequent latinisms, his explanation to his readers (almost contemptuously exaggerated) of Jewish purifications and distinctions of meats (vii. 3 *f.*), presupposition of the Roman form of divorce (x. 12), explanation in Roman money of the value of the (Greek and Oriental) " mite " (*lepton*), are well-known confirmations of the tradition of the writing's place of origin. But these are superficial characteristics. More important for us to note is the fundamental conception of what constitutes " the gospel," and the writer's attitude on questions of the relation of Jew and Gentile and the authority of the apostles and kindred of the Lord.

The most striking characteristic of Mark is that it aims to present the gospel *about* Jesus, and is relatively indifferent to the gospel *of* Jesus. Had the writer conceived his task after the manner of a Matthew there is little doubt that he could have compiled catechetic discourses of Jesus like the Sermon on the Mount or the discourse on prayer of Luke xi. 1–13. The fact that he disregards such records of Jesus' ethical and religious instruction does not mean that he (tacitly) refers his readers to the Matthæan Precepts, or similar compilations, to supplement his own deficiencies. It means a different, more Pauline, conception of what " the gospel " is. Mark conceives its primary element to be attachment to the *person* of Jesus, and has already gone far toward obliterating the primitive distinction between a Jesus whose earthly career had been " in great humility," and the glorified Son of God. The earthly Jesus is still, it is true, only a man endowed with the Spirit of Adoption. But he is so completely "in" the Spirit, and so fully endowed with it, as almost to assume the Greek figure of a demi-god treading the earth incognito. No wonder this Gospel became the favourite of the Adoptionists and Doketists.

Mark does not leave his reader in the dark as to what a man must do to inherit eternal life. The requirement does not appear until after Jesus has taken up with the twelve the road to Calvary, because it is distinctly *not* a keeping of commandments, new or old. It is an adoption of "the mind that was in Christ, who humbled himself and became obedient unto death." In Matthew's 'improved' version of Jesus' answer to the rich applicant for eternal life, the suppliant is told he may obtain it by obeying the commandments, with supererogatory merit ("if thou wouldest be perfect"), if he follows Jesus' example of self-abnegating service. In the form and context from which Matthew borrows (Mark x. 13–45) there is no trace of this legalism, and the whole idea of supererogatory merit, or higher reward, is strenuously, almost indignantly, repudiated. No man can receive the kingdom at all who does not receive it "as a little child." Every man must be prepared to make every sacrifice, even if he has kept all the commandments from his youth up. Peter and the disciples who have "left all and followed" are in respect to reward on the same level as others. Peter's plea for the twelve is answered, "There is no man that hath left" earthly possessions for Christ's sake that is not amply compensated even here. He must expect persecution now, but will receive eternal life hereafter. Only "many that are first shall be last, and last first." Even the martyr-apostles James and John will have no superior rights in the Kingdom.

Such passages as the above not only reveal why Mark's gospel shows comparative disregard of the Precepts, but also displays an attitude toward the growing claims of apostolic authority and neo-legalism which in contrast with Matthew and Luke is altogether refreshing. The kindred of the Lord appear but twice (iii. 20 *f*., 31–35 and vi. 1–6), both times in a wholly unfavourable light. "John appears but once, and that to receive a rebuke for intolerance. James and John appear only to be rebuked for selfish ambition. Peter seldom otherwise than for rebuke. All the disciples show constantly the blindness and "hardness of heart" which is explicitly said to characterize their nation (vi. 52; vii. 18; viii. 12, 14–21). Their self-seeking and unfaithfulness is the foil to Jesus' self-denial and faithfulness (viii. 33; ix. 6, 18 *f*., 29; x. 24, 28, 32, 37, 41; xiv. 27–31, 37–41, 50, 66–72). That which in Matthew (xvi. 16–19) has become a special divine revelation to Peter of the messiahship, marking the foundation of the church, is in the earlier Markan form (Mark viii. 27–33) not a revelation of the messiahship at all. Peter's answer, "Thou are the Christ," is common knowledge. The twelve are not supposed to be more ignorant than the demons! There is, however, a caustic rebuke of Peter for his carnal, Jewish idea of the implications of Christhood. A revelation of its significance almost Doketic in character is indeed granted just after to "Peter, James and John"; but they remain without appreciation or understanding of the 'vision,' though it exhibits Jesus in his heavenly glory in company with the translated heroes of the Old Testament. The revelation still remains, therefore, a sealed book until "after the resurrection."

This exaggeration of the disciples' obtuseness is partly due, no doubt, to apologetic motives. The evangelist has to meet the objection, If Jesus was really the extraordinary, superhuman being represented, and was openly proclaimed such by the evil spirits, why was nothing heard of his claims until after the crucifixion and alleged resurrection? His carrying back into the Galilean ministry of the glorified Being of Paul's redemption doctrine compels him to represent the twelve as sharing the dulness of the people who "having eyes see not, and having ears hear not." But with all allowance for this, the Roman Gospel shows small consideration for the apostles and kindred of the Lord.

It shows quite as little for Jewish prerogative and Jewish law. Jesus speaks in parables because to those "without" his preaching is to be intentionally a 'veiled' gospel (iv. 1–34). The Inheritance will be taken away from them and given to others (xii. 1–12). Priests and people together were guilty of the rejection and murder of Jesus (xv. 11–15, 29–32). Forgiveness of sins is offered by Jesus on his own authority in defiance of the scribes. Their exclusion of the publicans and sinners he disregards, proclaims abolition of their fasts, and holds their sabbath-keeping up to scorn (ii. 1—iii. 6). On the question of distinctions of meats his position is the most radical possible. The Jewish ceremonial is a "vain worship," mere "commandments of men." Defilement cannot be contracted by what "goes into a man." Jesus' saying about inward purity was not aimed at the mere 'hedge of the Law' (Matt. xv. 13), nor the mere matter of ablutions (Matt. xv. 20), but was intended to "make all meats clean" (vii. 1–23). Moses' law in some of its enactments does not represent the real divine will, but a human accommodation to human weakness (x. 2–9). Obedience to its highest code does not ensure eternal life (x. 19–21). The single law of love is "much more than all whole burnt offering and sacrifices" (xii. 28–34). When *all* the references to Judaism, its Law, its institutions, and its prerogative, are of this character, when Jesus *always* appears in radical opposition to the Law and its exponents (xii. 38–40; xiii. 1 *f.*), *never* as their supporter in any degree, the evangelist comes near to making it too hard for us to believe that he really was of Jewish birth.

On the other hand we cannot doubt the statement that he derives his anecdotes, however indirectly, from the preaching of Peter. The prologue (i. 1–13), indeed, makes no pretence of reporting the testimony of any witness, but acquaints the reader with the true nature of Jesus as " the Christ, the Son of God " by means of a mystical account of his baptism and endowment with the Spirit of Adoption, probably resting upon that document of Q, which we have distinguished from the Precepts. But the ensuing story of the ministry opens at the home of Peter in Capernaum, and continues more or less connected therewith in spite of interjected groups of anecdotes whose connection is not chronological but topical, such as ii. 1—iii. 6; iii. 22–30; iv. 1–34. It reaches its climax where Jesus at Cæsarea Philippi takes Peter into his confidence. Here again the mystical Revelation or Transfiguration vision (ix. 2–10) interrupts the connection, and shows its foreign derivation by the transcendental sense in which it interprets the person of Jesus. Certain features suggest its having been taken from the same source as the prologue (i. 1–13).

The story issues in the tragedy at Jerusalem, where, as before, Peter's figure, however unfavourable the contrast in which it is set to that of Jesus, is still the salient one. The outline in general is identical with that so briefly sketched in Acts x. 38–42—*except* that the absolutely essential point, the one thing which no gospel narrative can possibly have lacked, the resurrection manifestation to the disciples, and the commission to preach the gospel, is absolutely lacking!

That Mark's gospel once contained such a conclusion is almost a certainty. Imagine a gospel narrative without a report of the manifestation of the risen Lord to his disciples! Imagine a church—and that the church at *Rome*—giving out as the first, the authentic, original, and (in intention) the only account of the origin of the Christian faith (Mark i. 1), a narrative which *ended* with the apostles scattered in cowardly desertion, and Peter the most conspicuous, most remorseful renegade of them all! He who writes in Peter's name from Rome but shortly after, affectionately naming Mark "my son," must have had indeed a forgiving spirit. But traces of the real sequel have not all disappeared. Many outside allusions still remain to the turning again of Peter and stablishing of his brethren in the resurrection faith. The earliest is Paul's (1st Cor. xv. 5). The present Mark itself implies that it once had such an ending; for Jesus promises to rally his flock in Galilee after he is raised up (xiv. 28), and the women at the sepulchre are bidden to remind the disciples of the promise, though they fail to deliver their message. Indeed the whole Gospel looks forward to it. To this end "the mystery of the kingdom" is given to the chosen twelve (iii. 13 *f*., 31–35; iv. 10–12); for this they are forewarned (though vainly) of the catastrophe (viii. 34—ix. 1, 30–32; x. 32–34; xiv. 27–31). In fact the promise of a baptism of the Spirit (i. 8) probably implies that the original sequel related not only the appearance to Peter and (later) to the rest with the charge to preach, but also their endowment with the gifts, perhaps as in John xx. 19–23. What we now have is only a substitute for this original sequel, a substitute so ill-fitting as to have provoked repeated attempts at improvement.

From xvi. 8 onwards, as is well known, the oldest textual authorities have simply a blank. Later authorities give a shorter or longer substitute for the missing Manifestation and Charge to the twelve. The shorter follows Matthew, the longer follows Luke, with traces of acquaintance with John. Fanciful theories to explain these textual phenomena, such as accidental mutilation of the only copy, are improbable, and do not explain. If conjecture be permissible it is more likely that the original work was in two parts, after the manner of Luke–Acts, the 'former treatise' ending with the centurion's testimony, "Truly this man was a Son of God" (xv. 39). The second part continued the narrative in the form of a Preaching of Peter, perhaps ending with his coming to Rome; for the ancient literature of the church had several narratives of this type. Its disappearance will have been due to the superseding (perhaps the embodiment) of it by the work of Luke. When the primitive Markan 'former treatise' was adapted for separate use as a gospel it was quite natural that it should be supplemented (we can hardly say "completed") by the addition of the story of the Empty Sepulchre (xv. 40—xvi. 8), though this narrative is quite unknown to the primitive resurrection preaching (*cf.* 1st Cor. xv. 3–11), and one in which every character save Pilate is a complete stranger to the body of the work. The subsequent further additions of the so-called "longer" and "shorter" endings belong to the history of transcription after A.D. 140.

It will be apparent from the above that the Gospel of Mark is no exception to the rule that church-writings of this type inevitably undergo recasting and supplementation until the advancing process of canonization at last fixes their text with unalterable rigidity. Whether we recognize "sources," or earlier "forms," or only earlier "editions" of Mark, it is certain that appendices could still be attached long after the appearance of Luke, and probable that in the early period of its purely local currency at Rome the fund of Petrine anecdote had received more than one adaptation of form before it was carried to Syria and embodied substantially as we now have it in the composite gospels of Matthew and Luke. The omission by Luke of Mark vi. 45—viii. 26 is intentional,[1] and cannot be used to prove the existence of a shorter form; and the same is probably true of the omission of Mark ix. 38–40 by Matthew. Mark xii. 41–44, however, is probably an addition later than Matthew's time. Neither Matthew nor Luke had a text extending beyond xvi. 8. But signs of acquaintance with the original sequel appear in the appendix to John (John xxi.) and in the late and composite *Gospel of Peter* (*c.* 140). According to the latter the twelve remained in Jerusalem scattered and in hiding for the remaining six days of the feast. At its close they departed, mourning and grieving, each man to his own home. Peter and a few others, including "Levi the son of Alpheus," resumed their fishing "on the sea." . . . The fragment breaks off at this point. The story may be conjecturally completed from 1st Cor. xv. 5–8, with comparison of John xxi. 1–13; Luke v. 4–8; xxii. 31 *f.*; xxiv. 34, 36–43.

As we look back upon the undertaking of this humble author, named only by tradition, one among the catechists of the great church of Paul and Peter, writing but a few years after their death, but a few years before 1st Peter and Hebrews, one is struck by the grandeur of his aim. It is true he was not

[1] See below.

wholly without predecessors in the field. The work which afforded him at least the substance of his prologue, and in all probability other considerable sections of his book, had already aimed in a more mystical way to connect the Pauline doctrine of Christ as the Wisdom of God with the mighty works and teachings of Jesus. Duplication of a considerable part of Mark's story (vii. 31—viii. 26 repeats with some variation vi. 30—vii. 30) shows that his work was one of combination as well as creation. But outline, proportion and onward march of the story show not only skill and care, but large-minded and consistent adherence to the fundamental plan to tell the origin of the Christian faith (Mark i. 1).

Confirmation of the belief and practice of the church—it is for this that Mark reports all he can learn of the years of obscurity in Galilee followed by the tragedy in Jerusalem. Not only belief in Jesus as the Son of God will be justified by the story, but the founding, institutions, and ritual of the existing church. He manifestly adapts it to show not only the superhuman powers and attributes of the chosen Son of God, but the germ and type of all the church's institutions. Its baptism of repentance and accompanying gift of the Spirit of Adoption only repeats the experience of Jesus at the baptism of John. Endowment with the word of wisdom and the word of power is but the counterpart of Jesus' divine equipment with "the power of the Spirit" when he taught and healed in Galilee. The Sending of the Twelve sets the standard for the church's evangelists and missionaries, just as the Breaking of the Bread in Galilee gives the model for its fraternal banquet. So for the Judæan ministry as well. The path of martyrdom is that which all must follow, its Passover Supper of the Lord and Vigil in Gethsemane are models for the church's annual observance, its Passover of the Lord, its Vigil, its Resurrection feast. The grouping of the anecdotes is not all of Mark's doing, for we can still see in many cases how they have grown up around the church observances, to explain and justify the rites, rather than to form part of an outlined career. But taking the work as a whole, and considering how far beyond that of any other church was the opportunity at Rome, where Paul had transmitted the lofty conception of the Son of God, and Peter the concrete tradition of his earthly life, we cannot wonder that Mark's outline so soon became the standard account of Jesus' earthly ministry, and ultimately the only one.

But little space remains in which to trace the developments of gospel story in other fields. Southern Syria and Egypt soon found it needful, as we have seen, to adopt the work of Mark, but independently and as a framework for the Matthæan Precepts. It cannot have been long after that Antioch and Northern Syria followed suit. For Luke, though acquainted with the work of 'many' predecessors gives no sure evidence of acquaintance with Matthew. When we find such unsoftened contradictions as those displayed between these two Greek gospels in their opening and closing chapters, and observe, moreover, that while both indulge in hundreds of corrections and improvements upon Mark, these are rarely coincident and never make the assumption of interdependence necessary, it is hard to resist the conclusion that neither evangelist was directly acquainted with the other's work. Now no other gospel compares with Matthew in the rapidity and extent of its circulation, while Luke declares himself a diligent inquirer. He could not ignore the claims of apostolic authority to which this early and wide acceptance of Matthew were mainly due. The inference is reasonable that Luke's date was but little later than that of Matthew. If the probability of his employment of the *Antiquities* of Josephus could be raised to a certainty this would suffice to date the Gospel and Book of Acts not earlier than 96. Internal and external evidence, as judged by most scholars, converge on a date approximating 100.

The North-Syrian derivation of Luke–Acts is less firmly established in tradition than the Roman origin of Mark and the South-Syrian of Matthew. Ancient tradition can point to nothing weightier than the statement of Eusebius, drawn we know not whence, but independently made in the argumenta (prefixed descriptions) of several Vulgate manuscripts that Luke was of Antiochian birth. However, internal evidence supplies corroboration in rather unusual degree. If the reading of some texts in Acts xi. 28, "And as *we* were assembled," could be accepted, this alone would be almost conclusive corroboration. But dubious as it is, it furnishes support. For if an alteration of the original, it is at any rate extremely early (*c.* 150 ?) and aimed to support the belief in question.[1] Moreover the whole attitude of Luke–Acts in respect to apostolic authority, settlement of the great question of the terms of fellowship between Jew and Gentile, and description of the founding of the Pauline churches, is such as to make its origin anywhere between the Taurus range and the Adriatic most improbable; while if we place it in Rome we shall have an insoluble problem in the relation of its extreme emphasis on apostolic authority, and quasi-deification of Peter, to the stalwart independence of Mark. Conversely there are many individual traits which suggest Antioch as the place of origin. Next to Jerusalem, the never-to-be-forgotten church of "the apostles and elders," Antioch is the mother church of Christendom. There the name "Christian" had its origin. There the work of converting the Gentiles was begun. The

[1] Note, also, how in Acts vi. 5 the list of deacon-evangelists concludes "and Nicholas *a proselyte of Antioch*."

Greek churches of Cyprus and Asia Minor are regarded as dependencies of Antioch. Even those of the Greek peninsula are linked as well as may be to Antioch and Jerusalem, with suppression of the story of the schism. Antioch, not the Pauline Greek churches, is the benefactress of "the poor saints in Jerusalem," and at the instance of Antioch, by appeal to "the apostles and elders," the "decrees" are obtained which permanently settle the troublesome question of the obligation of maintaining ceremonial cleanness which still rests upon "the Jews which are among the Gentiles." As we have seen, the settlement is as far from that of Mark and the Pauline churches on the one side, as from the thoroughgoing legalism of Jerusalem on the other. As late as the Pastoral Epistles abstinence from "meats which God created to be received with thanksgiving by them that believe and know the truth" is to the Pauline churches a "doctrine of devils and seducing spirits" taught "through the hypocrisy of men that speak lies." Distinctions of meats belong to Jewish superstition, because "every creature of God is good and nothing is to be rejected, if it be received with thanksgiving" (1st Tim. iv. 1–5). Mark, as we have seen, takes precisely this standpoint. He is equally radical in condemning distinctions of meats as essentially "vain worship," and a "commandment of men" (Mark vii. 1–23). In truth if we distinguish one of Luke's *sources* from Luke himself we shall find exactly this doctrine taught to Peter himself by special divine revelation in Acts x. 10–16; xi. 3–10. Only, as we have already seen (p. 59, note), this is not the application made by the Book of Acts, as it now stands, of the material. To 'Luke' nothing could be more repugnant than the idea of an apostle forsaking the religion of his fathers, of which circumcision and "the customs" are an essential part. His cancellation, in the story of Peter's revelation and the Apostle's subsequent defence of it before the church in Jerusalem, of one of its essential factors, viz. the right to *eat* with Gentiles, regardless of man-made distinctions of meats ("what *God* hath cleansed make not *thou* common") is quite as significant as his restriction of even Paul's activity to Greek-speaking *Jews*, until "the Spirit" has expressly directed the church in Antioch, immediately after the persecution of Agrippa I, to proceed with the propaganda. Both alterations of the earlier form of the story are in line with a multitude of minor indications, and furnish us, in combination with them, the real keynote of the narrative. In Luke–Acts more clearly than in any of the gospels the writer assumes the distinctive function of the *historian*. He, too, would relate, like Mark, the origin of the Christian faith, and that "from the very first." He even deduces the pedigree of Jesus from "Adam, which was the son of God." But the object is far more to prove the pedigree of the faith than the pedigree of Jesus. Christianity is to be defended against the charge of being a *nova superstitio*, a *religio illicita*. On the contrary it is the one true and revealed religion, the perfect flower and consummation of Judaism. Yet it is not, like Judaism, particularistic and national, but universal; for while God at first made that nation the special repository of his truth, it was his "determinate foreknowledge and counsel" that they should reject and crucify their Messiah, making it possible to "proclaim this salvation unto the Gentiles." The one thing Luke is so anxiously concerned to prove that he wearies the reader with constant reiteration of it, proclaims it, argues it, in season and out of season, with his sources, against his sources, with the facts, against the facts, is that this faith was never, never, offered to the Gentiles except by express direction of God and after the Jews had demonstrated to the last extremity of stiff-necked opposition that they would have none of it. Christianity, then, and not Judaism, is the true primitive and revealed religion, the heir of all the divine promises.

We can see now why Luke finds it impossible to adopt Mark's story of a missionary journey of Jesus in "the coasts of Tyre and Sidon" and will not even mention the name of Cæsarea Philippi. His method in omitting Mark vi. 45—viii. 26 is more radical than Matthew's, but his motive is similar. The central theme of this portion of Mark appears in the chapter (ch. vii.) recording Jesus' repudiation of the Jewish distinctions of clean and unclean as "precepts of men," and departing to heal and preach in Phœnicia and Decapolis. This is the theme of Luke's second treatise; and, as we have seen, his solution of the problem is radically different. If he cannot admit that even Paul disregarded "the customs" or Peter preached to Gentiles until after express and reiterated direction of "the Spirit," we surely ought not to expect him to admit the statement that Jesus repudiated the distinctions of Mosaism, declared "all meats clean," and departing into the coasts of Tyre and Sidon first healed the daughter of "a Gentile" and afterward continued his journey "through Sidon" and "the regions of Decapolis," repeating the symbolic miracles of opening deaf ears and blind eyes, and feeding with loaves and fishes. Even if this supposed ministry of Jesus among the Gentiles stood on a much stronger foundation of historical probability than is unfortunately the case (*cf.* Rom. xv. 8), it could not logically be admitted to the work of Luke without an abandonment of one of his firmest convictions and a rewriting of both his treatises.

Luke was probably not the first to divide his work into a "former treatise" covering "both" the sayings and doings of Jesus "until the time that he was taken up," and a second devoted to the work of the apostles after they had received the charge to proclaim the gospel "to the uttermost parts of the earth." "Many," as he tells us, had already undertaken to "draw up narratives" (*diegeses*) of this kind, of which the one Luke himself has chiefly employed, had originally, as we concluded, a sequel like his own Book of Acts. There are even features of the Petrine souree of Acts which particularly connect it with Roman doctrine (*e. g.* Acts x. 10–15; *cf.* Rom. xiv. 14 and Mark vii. 18 *f.*) and even with the person of Mark (Acts xii. 12). Its balance between Peter and Paul and its close with the establishment of Christianity at Rome, are also suggestive that the greater part of Luke's second treatise came *ultimately* from the same source as his first. But the division of the work into two parts: (1) the gospel among the Jews; (2) the gospel among the Gentiles, would have followed, independently of any such precedent, from the whole purpose and structure of the work. Christianity is to be proved in the light of its origin, and in spite of the hostility of the Jews among whom it arose, and whose sacred writings it adopts, to be the original, true, revealed religion. To prove this it must be shown that the rejection and crucifixion of Jesus by his own people as a result of his earthly ministry was due not to his own failure to meet the ideal of the Scriptures in question, but to *their* perversity and wilful blindness. If it is important to prove in the former treatise that the opposition of the controlling authorities among the Jews was due to this perversity and jealousy, it is at least equally so to show that the lowly and devout received him gladly. Hence the peculiar hospitality of Luke toward material showing Jesus' acceptance of and by the humbler and the outcast classes, the poor and lowly, women, Samaritans, publicans and sinners. The idyllic scenes of his birth and childhood are cast among men and women of this type of Old Testament piety, quietly "waiting for the kingdom of God." During his career it is these who receive and hang upon him. Even on Calvary *one* of the thieves must join with this throng of devout and penitent believers. Jesus' preaching begins with his rejection by his own fellow-townsmen only because "no prophet is accepted in his own country"; though before their attempt to slay him he proves from Scripture how Elijah and Elisha had been sent unto the Gentiles. His ministry ends with his demonstration to the disciples after his resurrection from "Moses and all the prophets" how that "it was needful that the Christ should suffer before entering his glory," and that after his rejection by Israel "repentance and remission of sins should be preached in his name among all nations, beginning at Jerusalem."

The second treatise shows how this purpose

of God to secure the dissemination of the true faith by the disobedience and hardening of its first custodians was accomplished, chief stress being always laid upon the fact that it was only when the Jews "contradicted and blasphemed" that the apostles said, "It was necessary that the word of God should first be spoken to you, but seeing ye put it from you, and judge yourselves unworthy of eternal life, lo, we turn to the Gentiles." There is no interest taken in the subsequent fortunes of Jerusalem and Jewish Christianity, nor even in the fate of Peter and James, after this transition has been effected to Gentile soil. There is no interest taken in the spread of Christianity as such, in Egypt, Ethiopia, Cyrenaica, Cyprus, Mesopotamia; but only where the conflict rages over the respective claim of Jew and Gentile to be the true heir of the promises, *i. e.* the mission-field of Paul. At the individual centres the story goes just far enough to relate how the gospel was offered to the Jews and rejected, compelling withdrawal from the synagogue, and thereafter it is told over again with slight variations at the next centre. The book concludes with a repetition of the stereotyped scene at Rome itself, in spite of the representation of the very source employed, that an important church had long existed there before Paul's coming, ending with a quotation of the classic passage from Isa. vi. 9 *f.* to prove God's original purpose to harden the heart of Israel, so that his "salvation might be sent unto the Gentiles." The very fate of Paul himself has so little interest for Luke in comparison with this demonstration of Christianity as the one original, revealed religion, enclosed in Judaism as seeds are confined in the hardening seed-pod until disseminated by its bursting, that he leaves it unmentioned, like that of all other leaders of the church whose death was not directly contributory to the process.

Many, and vitally important to the development of Gospel Story as we know it, as were the sources of Luke, both by his own statement (Luke i. 1) and the internal evidences of his work, he has made analysis extremely difficult by the skilful and elaborate stylistic embroidery with which he has overlaid the gaps and seams. Nor is this a proper occasion for entering the field of the higher critic. Luke–Acts represents the completed development, not the naïve beginnings of this type of the Literature of the Church Teacher. We have seen reason to think we may have traces of the earlier "narratives" (*diegeses*) to which Luke refers, not only in the great Roman work of Mark, but in a part of the Q material itself. If Antioch were the place of origin of this early source, if here too were found those archives of missionary activity whence came the famous Diary employed in Acts xvi.–xxviii., the contribution of this church to Gospel Story was such as to make Antioch the appropriate centre for the great "historical" school of interpretation of the fourth and fifth centuries. When we consider the dominant motive of Luke and his extraordinary exaltation of 'apostolic' authority we seem to be breathing the very atmosphere of Ignatius the great apostle of ecclesiasticism and apostolic order, discipline and succession. Ignatius' hatred of Doketism, too, is not without a certain anticipation in the opening and closing chapters of Luke's Gospel, and perhaps in the fact that the great exsection from Mark begins with the story of the Walking on the Sea (Mark vi. 45–52).

CHAPTER VIII

THE JOHANNINE TRADITION. PROPHECY

IN Paul's enumeration of the "gifts" by which the Spirit qualifies various classes of men to build in various ways upon the structure of the church, the class of "prophets" takes the place next after that of "apostles," a rank even superior (as more manifestly 'spiritual') to that of "pastors and teachers." The Book of Acts shows us as its most conspicuous centre of "prophecy" the house of Philip the Evangelist at Cæsarea. This man had four unmarried daughters who prophesied, and in his house Paul received a 'prophetic' warning of his fate from a certain Agabus who had come down from Judæa. There were also prophets in Antioch (Acts xiii. 1), though the only ones mentioned by name are this same Agabus [1] and Silas, or Silvanus, who is also from Judæa. In the *Teaching of the Twelve* the 'prophet' still appears among the regular functionaries of the church, for the most part a traveller from

[1] The mention of Agabus, however, in xi. 27*f.* is hardly consistent with xiii. 1 and xxi. 10–14. It seems to be due to the editorial recasting of xi. 22–30.

place to place, and open to more or less suspicion, as is the case at Rome, where Hermas combines reverence for the "angel" that speaks through the true prophet, with warnings against the self-seeker. In 1st John the "false prophets" are a serious danger, propagating Doketic heresy wherever they go. In fact, this heresy was, as we know, the great peril in Asia. However, Asia, if plagued by wandering false prophets, had also become by this time a notable seat of true and authentic prophecy; for the same Papias who shows such sympathy with Polycarp against those who were "perverting the Sayings of the Lord to their own lusts," and had turned, as Polycarp advised, "to the tradition handed down from the beginning," had similar means for counteracting those who "denied the resurrection and judgment." Among those upon whom he principally relied as exponents of the apostolic doctrine were two of those same prophesying daughters of Philip the Evangelist, who with their father had migrated from Cæsarea Palestina to Hierapolis, leaving, however, one, who had married, a resident till her death at Ephesus. As late as the time of Montanus (150–170), the "Phrygians" traced their succession of prophets and prophetesses back to Silvanus and the daughters of Philip.

We cannot be sure that the traditions Papias reported from these prophetesses were derived at first hand, though it is not impossible that Papias himself may have seen them. However it is certain that many of his traditions of 'the Elders' had to do with eschatology, and aimed to prove the material and concrete character of the rewards of the kingdom; for we have several examples of these traditions, attributing to Jesus apocryphal descriptions of the marvellous fertility of Palestine in the coming reign of Messiah, and particularizing about the abodes of the blessed. Moreover Eusebius blames Papias for the crude ideas of Irenæus and other second century fathers who held the views called "chiliastic" (*i. e.* based on the "thousand" year reign of Christ in Rev. xx. 2 *f.*). We also know that Papias defended the "trustworthiness" of Revelation, a book which served as the great authority of the "chiliasts" for the next fifty years in their fight against the deniers of the resurrection. He quoted from it, in fact, the passage above referred to; so that if reason must be sought for his placing "John and Matthew" together at the end of his list of seven apostles instead of in their usual place, it is probably because they were his ultimate apostolic authorities for the "word of prophecy" and for the "commandment of the Lord" respectively. Justin Martyr, Papias' contemporary at Rome, though converted in Ephesus, and unquestionably determined in his mould of thought by Asiatic Paulinism, has, like Papias, but two *authorities* for his gospel teaching: (1) the commandment of the Lord represented in the

Petrine and Matthæan tradition; (2) prophecy, represented in the Christian continuation of the Old Testament gift. This second authority, however, is not appealed to without the support of apostolicity. Revelation is quoted as among "our writings," like "the memorabilia of the apostles called Gospels," but not without the additional assurance that the seer was "John, one of the *apostles* of Christ."

For 'prophecy,' however acclimated elsewhere, was in its origin distinctively a Palestinian product. Its stock in trade was Jewish eschatology as developed in the long succession of writers of 'apocalypse' since Daniel (165 B.C.). Of the nature of this curious and fantastic type of literature we have seen some examples in 2nd Thessalonians and the Synoptic eschatology (Mark xiii.=Matt. xxiv.= Luke xxi.). More can be learned by comparing the contemporary Jewish writings of this type known as 2nd Esdras and the Apocalypse of Baruch. Older examples are found in the prophecies and visions purporting to come from Enoch. For apocalypse became the successor of true prophecy in proportion as the loss of Israel's separate national existence and the enlargement of its horizon compelled it to make its messianic hopes transcendental, and its notion of the Kingdom cosmic. Hence comes all the phantasmagoria of allegorical monsters, spirits and demons, the great conflict no longer against Assyria and Babylon, but a war of the powers of light and darkness, heaven and hell. Yet all centres still upon Jerusalem as the ultimate metropolis of the world, whose empires, now given over to the leadership of Satan, will soon lie prostrate beneath her feet.

Some such eschatology of divine judgment and reward is an almost necessary complement to the legalistic type of religion. If Christianity be conceived as a system of commandments imposed by supernatural authority it must have as a motive for obedience a system of supernatural rewards and punishments. Not merely, then, because for centuries the legalism of the scribes had actually had its corresponding development of apocalypse, with visions of the great judgment and Day of Yahweh, but because of an inherent and necessary affinity between the two, "Judæa" continued to be the home of 'prophecy' in New Testament times also.

However, the one great example of this type of literature that has been (somewhat reluctantly) permitted to retain a place in the New Testament canon appears at first blush to be clearly and distinctively a product of Ephesus. Of no book has early tradition so clear and definite a pronouncement to make as of Revelation. Since the time of Paul the Jewish ideas of resurrection provoked opposition in the Greek mind. The Greek readily accepted immortality, but the crudity of Jewish millenarianism, with its return of the dead from the grave for a visible, concrete rule of Messiah in Palestine repelled him. The representation of Acts xvii. 32 is fully borne out by the constant effort of Paul in his Greek epistles to remove the stumbling-blocks of this doctrine. It is no surprise, then, to find the 'prophecy' of Revelation, and more particularly its doctrine of the thousand-year reign of Messiah in Jerusalem, a subject of dispute at least since Melito of Sardis (167), and probably since Papias (145). Fortunately controversy brought out with unusual definiteness, and from the earliest times, positive statements regarding the origin of the book. Irenæus (186) declared it a work of the Apostle John given him in vision "in the end of the reign of Domitian." The same date (93), may be deduced from statements of Epiphanius regarding the history of the church in Thyatira. Justin Martyr (153), as we have seen, vouches for the crucial passage (Rev. xx. 2 *f.*) as from "one of ourselves, John, an apostle of the Lord." Papias (145) vouched for its orthodoxy at least, if not its authenticity. There can be no reasonable doubt that it came to be accepted in Asia early in the second century, in spite of opposition, as representing the authority of the Apostle John, and as having appeared there *c.* 95. In fact, there is no book of the entire New Testament whose external attestation can compare with that of Revelation, in nearness, clearness, definiteness, and positiveness of statement. John is as distinctively the father of 'prophecy' in second century tradition as Matthew of 'Dominical Precepts' and Peter of 'Narratives.'

Moreover the book itself purports to be written from Patmos, an island off the coast of Asia. It speaks in the name of "John" as of some very high and exceptional authority, well known to all the seven important churches addressed, the first of which is "Ephesus." By its references to local names and conditions it even proves, in the judgment of all the most eminent modern scholars, that it really did see the light for the first time (at least for the first time in its present form) in Ephesus not far from A.D. 95.

One would think the case for apostolic authenticity could hardly be stronger. And yet no book of the New Testament has had such difficulty as this, whether in ancient or modern times, to maintain its place in the canon. It must also be said that no book gives stronger internal evidence of having passed through at least two highly diverse stages in process of development to its present form.

The theory of "another John" is indeed comparatively modern. Nobody dreamed of such a solution until Dionysius of Alexandria hesitatingly advanced the conjecture in his controversy with Nepos the Chiliast. Even then (*c.* 250) Dionysius (though he must have known the little work of Papias) could think of no other John at Ephesus than the Apostle, unless it were perhaps John Mark! It is Eusebius who joyfully helps him out with the discovery in Papias of "John the Elder." But Eusebius himself is candid enough to admit that Papias only quoted "traditions of John" and "mentioned him frequently in his writings." When we read Papias' own words, though they are cited by Eusebius for the express purpose of proving the debatable point, it is obvious that they prove nothing of the kind, but rather imply the contrary, viz. that John the Elder, though a contemporary of Papias, was not accessible, but known to him only at second hand, by report of travellers who "came his way." In short, as we have seen, "Aristion and John the Elder" were the surviving members of a group of 'apostles, elders and witnesses of the Lord' in Jerusalem. If, then, one chose to attribute the 'prophecies' of Rev. iv.–xxi. to this Elder there could be no serious objections on the score of doctrine, for the "traditions of John" reported by Papias were not lacking in millenarian colour. Only, it is not the 'prophecies' of Rev. iv.–xxi. which contain the references to "John," but the enclosing prologue and epilogue; and these concern themselves with the churches of Asia as exclusively as the 'prophecies' with the quarrel of Jerusalem with Rome.

The second century is, as we have seen, unanimous in excluding from consideration any other John in Asia save the Apostle, and if the writer of Rev. i. and xxii. produced this impression in all contemporary minds without exception, including even such as opposed the book and its doctrine, it is superlatively probable that such was his intention. The deniers of the resurrection and judgment did not point out to Polycarp, Papias, Justin, Melito and Caius, that they were confusing two Johns, attributing the work of a mere Elder to the Apostle. They plumply declared the attribution to John fictitious; and since the internal evidence from the condition of the churches and growth of heresy in chh. i.–iii. and the imperial succession down to Domitian in chh. xiii. and xvii. strongly corroborate the date assigned in antiquity (*c.* 93), we have no alternative, if we admit that the Apostle John had long before been "killed by the Jews,"[1] but to suppose that this book, like nearly all the books of 'prophecy,' is, indeed, pseudonymous. It does not follow that he who assumes the name of "John" in prologue and epilogue (i. 1 *f.*, 4, 9; xxii. 8) to tell the reader definitely who the prophet is, was guilty of intentional misrepresentation. If anything can be made clear by criticism it is clear that the prophecies were not his own. They were taken from some nameless source. The "pseudonymity" consists simply in clothing a conjecture with the appearance of indubitable fact.

But why should a writer who wished to

[1] See above, p. 104.

clothe with apostolic authority the 'prophecies' he was promulgating, not assume boldly the title of "apostle," as the author of 2nd Peter has done in adapting similarly the Epistle of Jude? Why, if he assumes the name of the martyred Apostle John at all, does he refrain from saying, "I John, an *apostle*, or *disciple of the Lord*," and content himself with the humbler designation and authority of 'prophet'?

This question brings us face to face with the most remarkable structural phenomena of the book, and cannot be understandingly answered until we have considered them.

The outstanding characteristic of Revelation is its adaptation of literary material dealing with, and applicable to, one historical and geographical situation, to another situation almost completely different. The opening chapters, devoted to "John's" vision on Patmos and the conditions and dangers of the seven Churches of Asia, employ indeed some of the expressions of the substance of the book. The promises of the Spirit to the churches recall the glories of the New Jerusalem of the concluding vision of the seer. There is some reference to local persecution at Smyrna incited by the Jews ("a synagogue of Satan") and which is to last "ten days," and there is an isolated reference to a martyrdom of days long gone by in the message to the church in Pergamum (ii. 13) recalling remotely the blood and suffering of which the body of the work is full. This we should of course expect from an adapter of existing 'prophecies.' But the converse, *i. e.* consideration for the historical conditions of Ephesus and its sister churches, on the part of the body of the work, is absolutely wanting. On the one side is the situation of the Pauline churches on the east coast of the Ægean in A.D. 93–95. The prologue and epilogue (Rev. i.–iii. and xxii. 6–21) are concerned with these churches of Asia, and their development in the faith, particularly their growth in good works, purity from defilements of the world, and resistance to the inroads of heretical teaching. The message of the Spirit, conveyed through "John," is meant to encourage the members of these churches to pure living in the face of temptations to worldliness and impurity. The epistles to the churches, in a word, belong in the same class with the Pastorals, Jude, and 2nd Peter, as regards their object and the situation confronted; though they are written to enclose apocalyptic visions which deal with a totally different situation.

The visions, on the contrary, take not the smallest notice of (proconsular) Asia and its problems. Their scene is Palestine, their subject the outcome of Jerusalem's agonizing struggle against Rome. From the moment the threshold of iv. 1 is crossed there is no consciousness of the existence of such places as Ephesus, Smyrna and Thyatira. The scenes are Palestinian. The great battle-field is Har-Magedon (*i. e.* city of Megiddo, on the plain of Esdraelon, the scene of Josiah's overthrow, 2nd Kings xxiii. 29 *f.*). "The city," "the great city," "the holy city" is Jerusalem; though "spiritually (in allegory) it is called Sodom and Egypt" (*i. e.* a place from which the saints escape to avoid its doom). When the saints flee from the oppression of the dragon it is to "the wilderness." When the invading hordes rush in it is from beyond "the Euphrates." When the redeemed appear in company with the Christ it is on Mount Zion; they constitute an army of 144,000, twelve thousand from each of the twelve tribes. Two antagonistic powers are opposed. On the one side is Jerusalem and its temple, now given over to the Gentiles to be trodden under foot forty and two months, on the other is Rome, no longer, as with Paul, a beneficent and protecting power, but the city of the beast, Babylon the great harlot, at whose impending judgment the Gentiles will mourn, but all the servants of God rejoice. Jerusalem rebuilt, glorified, the metropolis of the world, seat and residence of God and his Christ, will take the place of Rome, the seat of the beast and the false prophet. The gates of this New Jerusalem will stand open to receive tribute from all the Gentile nations, and will have on them the names of the twelve tribes of Israel. The foundations of the city wall will have on them "the names of the twelve apostles of the Lamb."

All this is cumulative proof that the horizon of the seer of Rev. iv.–xx. is that of Palestine. Its expansion in the introductory Letters of the Spirit to the Churches to include the seven churches of (pro-consular) Asia, is as limited in its way as the original. The later writer merely adds the special province where he wishes the 'prophecy' to circulate, with its special interests; there is no real inter-relation of the two parts.

It is a problem of great complexity to disentangle the various strands of this strange and fantastic work, certain as it is that we have here a conglomerate whose materials come from various periods. Some elements, such as ch. xi. on the fate of Jerusalem, seem to date in part from before 70; others, such as ch. xviii. on the fate of Rome, show that while originally composed for the circumstances of the reign of Vespasian or Titus, the time has been extended to take in at least the beginning of that of Domitian.[1] The author rests mainly upon the Hebrew apocalyptic prophets, such as Ezekiel, Daniel and Enoch, but he has not been altogether inhospitable to such originally Gentile mythology as the doctrine of the seven spirits of God, and the conflict of Michael and his angels with the dragon. He intimates himself that his prophesying had not been confined to one period or one people (x. 11). When he translates the "Hebrew" name of the angel of the abyss,

[1] Note the addition of an "eighth" emperor in ver. 11.

"Abaddon," into its Greek equivalent (ix. 11), or uses Hebrew numerical equivalents for the letters of the name of a man (xiii. 18), it is not difficult to guess that this prophecy had at least its origin in Palestine. In fact, there is no other country where the geographical references hold true, and no other period save that shortly after the overthrow of Jerusalem by Titus, that affords the historical situation here presupposed, when worshipping "the beast and his image" is demanded of the saints by the earthly ruler (Domitian), and the overthrow of the seven-hilled city by one of its own rulers in league with lesser powers is looked forward to as about to avenge the sufferings inflicted on the Jews. As regards this hope of the overthrow of Rome, we know that the legend of Nero's prospective return at the head of hosts of Parthian enemies to recapture his empire gained currency in Asia Minor in Domitian's reign, and this legend is certainly developed in Rev. xiii. and xvii. On the other hand, the author, if he ever came to Asia, did not cease to be a Palestinian Jew. He operates exclusively (after iv. 1) with the materials and interests of Jewish and Jewish-Christian apocalypse. He has no interest whatever in the churches of Asia. He does not betray by one syllable a knowledge even of their existence, to say nothing of their dangers, their heresies, their temptations. He does make it abundantly clear that he is a Christian prophet (x. 7–11), and (to us) almost equally clear that he is *not* one of the twelve apostles whose names he sees written on the foundation-stones of the New Jerusalem (xxi. 14). But since his prophecy, with all its heterogeneous elements had to do with the final triumph of Messiah, and the establishment of His kingdom, after the overthrow of the power of Satan—since it depicted "the time of the dead to be judged, and the time to give their reward to thy servants the prophets, and to the saints and to them that fear thy name," it could not fail to be welcomed by orthodox Christians in (proconsular) Asia. For the churches of Asia were engaged at this time in a vigorous struggle against the heretical deniers of the resurrection and judgment. Only, a mere anonymous prophecy from Palestine could not obtain any authoritative currency in Asia. To be accepted, even among the orthodox, some name of apostolic weight must be attached to it, as we see in the case of the two Epistles of Peter and those of James and Jude. The Epistles of the Spirit to the churches are, then, as truly "letters of commendation" as though they introduced a living prophet and not merely a written prophecy. The John whom they present is not called an apostle for the very simple reason that the visions themselves everywhere refer to their recipient as a 'prophet.' The author of the prologue and epilogue does not disregard the language of his material. As we have seen, he carefully weaves its phraseology into the 'letters.' So with his insertion of the name "John." It occurs nowhere but in i. 1 *f*., 4, 9 and xxii. 8 *f*. All these passages, but especially xxii. 8 *f*., are based upon xix. 9*b*, 10, adding nothing to the representation but the name "John" and the location "Patmos." In fact, xxii. 6–9 reproduces xix. 9 *f*., for the most part verbatim, although it is clearly insupposable that the seer of the former passage should represent himself as offering a *second* time to worship the angel, and as receiving *again* exactly the same rebuke he had received so shortly before. He who calls himself "John" in xxii. 8 is, therefore, *not* the prophet of xix. 10. The epilogue itself has apparently received successive supplements, and the prologue its prefix; but he who inserts the name John has done so with caution. He may not have intended to leave open the ambiguity found by Dionysius and Eusebius between the Apostle and the Elder, as a refuge in case of accusation, but he has at least been careful not to transgress the limits of the text he reproduces. The seer spoke of himself as a "*prophet*" writing from the midst of great *tribulation*, about the *kingdom* to follow to those that *endured*. He had said that he received "true *words of God*" from an *angel* who declared "I am a fellow *servant* with thee and with thy *brethren* that hold *the testimony of Jesus*" (*i. e.* the confession of martyrdom). The prologue, accordingly, describes "John" as a *servant* of Jesus, who received from an *angel* the *word of God* and *the testimony of Jesus* (i. 1 *f.*). He is a *brother* and partaker in the *tribulation* and *kingdom* and *endurance* which are in Jesus. When he comes to Asia it is "for the *word of God* and *the testimony of Jesus.*" The spot whence he issues his prophetic message is not located in Ephesus, or in any city where the residents could say, "But the Apostle John was never among us." He resides temporarily (as a prisoner in the quarries ?) in the unfrequented island of Patmos. Thence he could be supposed to see "in the Spirit" the condition of affairs in the churches of Asia without inconvenient questions as to when, and how, and why.

We may think, then, of this book of 'prophecy' as brought forth in the vicinity of Ephesus near "the end of the reign of Domitian" (95). But only the enclosing letters to the churches, and the epilogue guaranteeing the contents, originate here at this time. The 'prophecies,' occupied as they are exclusively with the rivalry of Jerusalem and Rome, and the judgment to be executed for the former upon her ruthless adversary, bear unmistakable marks of their Palestinian origin, not only in the historical and geographic situations presupposed, but in the "defiant" Hebraisms of the language, and the avowed translations from "the Hebrew." They are an importation from

Palestine like "the sound words, even the words of the Lord Jesus" referred to in the Pastorals. The churches of Asia are feeling the need of apostolic authority against the deniers of the resurrection and the judgment, as much as against the perverters of the Lord's words. Such centres as the homes of the prophesying daughters of Philip at Ephesus and Hierapolis were even more abundantly competent to supply this demand than the other. Agabus will not have been the only Judæan prophet who visited them, especially after the "great tribulation" which befell "those in Judæa." There is nothing foreign to the habit of the times, even in Christian circles, if nameless 'prophecies' from such a source are translated, edited, and given out under cover of commendatory epistles written in the name of "John" at a time when John had indeed partaken both of the tribulation and of the kingdom of Jesus. They would hardly have obtained currency had they not been attributed to an apostle; for a denial of the apostolicity of this book has always deprived it of authority.

On the other hand, the actual (Palestinian) prophet has no such exalted opinion of himself as of those whose names he sees written on the foundation of the walls of the New Jerusalem (xxi. 14). He is not an apostle and does not claim to be. He shows not the faintest trace of any association with the earthly Jesus, and indeed displays a vindictiveness toward the enemies of Israel that has more of the spirit of the imprecatory psalms than the spirit of Jesus. He thinks of Jesus as a king and judge bestowing heavenly rewards upon the martyrs in a manner quite inconsistent with his rebuke of James and John (Mark x. 40). It is a far cry indeed from this to apostleship and personal intimacy with Jesus.

The chief value of Revelation to the student of Christian origins is that by means of its clearly determinable date (Ephesus, 93–95) he can place himself at a point of vantage whence to look not only around him at the conditions of the Pauline churches as depicted in the letters, vexed with growing Gnostic heresy and moral laxity, but also both backward and forward. The backward glance shows Palestine emerging from the horrors of the Jewish war, filled with bitterness against Rome, held down under hateful tyranny and longing for vengeance upon the despot with his " names of blasphemy " and his demands of worship for " the image of the beast " (emperor-worship). Here Jewish apocalyptic (as in 2nd Esdras) and Christian 'prophecy' are closely in accord. Indeed a considerable part of the material of Rev. iv.–xxi., especially in chh. xi.–xii. is ultimately of Jewish rather than Christian origin. What the development of Christian 'prophecy' was in Palestine from apostolic times until the scattering of the church of " the apostles and elders" after the war of Bar Cocheba (135), we can only infer from the kindred Jewish apocalypses and the chiliastic "traditions of the Elders" quoted by Irenæus from Papias. A forward look from our vantage point in Ephesus *c.* A.D. 95, shows the effects of the Palestinian importation extending down from generation to generation, first in the long chiliastic controversy against the Doketic Gnostics, including Montanist 'prophecy'; secondly, in the growth of a claim to apostolic succession from John.

(1) In the chiliastic controversy for a century the chief bones of contention are the (non-Pauline) doctrine of the resurrection of the *flesh* (so the Apostles' Creed and the second-century fathers), and that of a visible reign of Christ for a thousand years in Jerusalem. The new form of resurrection-gospel which at about this time begins to take the place of the apostolic of 1st Cor. xv. 3–11, centering upon the emptiness of the sepulchre and the tangibility and food-consuming functions of Jesus' resurrection body, instead of the "manifestations" to the apostles, is characteristic of this struggle against the Greek disposition to spiritualize. Luke and Ignatius represent the attitude of the orthodox, Ignatius' opponents that of those who denied that Jesus was "in the flesh after his resurrection." Revelation, like the "traditions of the Elders," champions the visible kingdom of Messiah in Jerusalem.

(2) In the effort for apostolic authority the writings which came ultimately to represent Asian orthodoxy have all been brought under the name and authority of the Apostle John, although for many decades after the appearance of Revelation, Paul, and not John, remains the apostolic authority to which appeal is made, and although the writings themselves were originally anonymous. There was, indeed, a contributory cause for the growth of this tradition in the accidental circumstance that a Palestinian Elder from whom Papias derived indirect, and Polycarp in all probability direct, traditions, bore also the name of John, and survived until A.D. 117. Still, the main reason why this particular apostolic name was ultimately placed over the Gospel and Epistles of Ephesian Christendom, can only have been its previous adoption to cover the compilation of Palestinian 'prophecies' of A.D. 95.

PART IV

THE LITERATURE OF THE THEOLOGIAN

CHAPTER IX

THE SPIRITUAL GOSPEL AND EPISTLES

ASIA, as we have come to know it through a succession of writings dating from Colossians–Ephesians (*c.* 62) down to Papias (145), had come to be the chief scene of mutual reaction between 'apostolic' and Pauline Christianity at the close of the first century. Here at Ephesus had been the great headquarters of Paul's missionary activity. Here he had reasoned daily in the school of one Tyrannus, a philosopher, and had found "many adversaries." Here he had encountered the "strolling Jews, exorcists," and had secured the destruction of an immense mass of books of magic. Here, according to Acts, he predicted the inroads of heresy after his "departure," and here the succeeding literature abundantly witnesses the fulfilment of the prediction. Ephesians and Colossians begin the series, the Pastoral Epistles (*c.* 90) continue it. Then follow the 'letters to the churches' of Revelation (95) and the Ignatian Epistles (110–117), not to mention those whose origin is uncertain, such as Jude and 2nd Peter.

The Pastorals already make it apparent that even the Pauline churches are not exempt from the inevitable tendency of the age to fall back upon authority. The very sublimity of Paul's consciousness of apostolic inspiration made it the harder for the next generation to assert any for itself. Moreover heresy was growing apace. If even the outward pressure of persecution tended to drive the churches together in brotherly sympathy, still more indispensable would appear the need of traditional standards to maintain the "type of sound doctrine," "the faith once for all delivered to the saints." Without such it would be impossible to check the individualism of errorists who took Paul's sense of personal inspiration and mystical insight as their model, *without* Paul's sobriety of critical control under the standard of "the law of Christ." It is no surprise, then, to find even at the headquarters of Paulinism early in the second century a sweeping tendency to react toward the 'apostolic' standards. In particular, as Gnostic exaggeration of the Pauline mysticism led continually further toward disregard of the dictates of common morality, and a wider divergence from the Jewish conceptions of the world to come, it was natural that men like Polycarp and

Papias should turn to the Matthæan and Petrine tradition of the Lord's oracles, and to the Johannine 'prophecies' regarding the resurrection and judgment.

Had nothing intervened between Gnostics and reactionaries the most vital elements of Paul's gospel might well have disappeared, even at this great headquarters of Paulinism. The Doketists, with their exaggerated Hellenistic mysticism, were certainly not the true successors of Paul. They showed an almost contemptuous disregard for the historic Jesus, a one-sided aim at personal redemption, by mystic union of the individual soul with the Christ-spirit, to the disregard of "the law of Christ," even in some cases of common morality. Paul was characterized by a splendid loyalty to personal purity, to the social ideal of the Kingdom, and to the unity of the brotherhood in the spirit of reciprocal service. On the other hand men like the author of the Pastoral Epistles, Ignatius and Polycarp, with their almost panic-stricken resort to the authority of the past, were not perpetuating the true spirit of the great Apostle. Their reliance was on ecclesiastical discipline, concrete and massive miracle in the story of Jesus, particularly on the point of the bodily—or, as they would have said, the "fleshly"—resurrection. Their conception of his recorded "words," made of them a fixed, superhuman standard and rule, a "new law." Teachers of this type, much as they desired and believed themselves to be perpetuating the "sacred deposit" of Paul, were in reality conserving its form and missing its spirit. Such men would gladly "turn to the tradition handed down," of the Matthæan Sayings, and the Petrine Story. But in the former they would not find reflections of the sense of sonship. They would find only a supplementary Law, a new and higher set of rules. In the story they would not discover the Pauline view of the pre-existent divine Wisdom tabernacling in man, producing a second Adam, as elder brother of a new race, the children and heirs of God. They would take the mysticism of Paul and bring it down to the level of the man in the street. Jesus would be to them either a completely superhuman man, approximating the heathen demi-god, a divinity incognito; or else a man so endowed with "the whole fountain of the Spirit" as to exercise perpetually and uninterruptedly all its miraculous functions. The story of the cross would be hidden behind the prodigies.

Least of all could the importation of apocalyptic prophecy do justice to the Pauline doctrine of the 'last things.' True, Paul is himself a 'prophet,' thoroughly imbued with the fantastic Palestinian doctrines. He, too, believes in a world-conflict, a triumph of the Messiah over antichrist. More particularly in one of his very earliest epistles (2nd Thessalonians) we get a glimpse into these

Jewish peculiarities. But these are always counterbalanced in Paul by a wider and soberer view, which tends more and more to get the upper hand. His doctrine of spiritual union with Christ, present apprehension of "the life that is hid with Christ in God," a doctrine of Greek rather than Hebrew parentage, prevails over the imagery of Jewish apocalypse. In the later epistles he expects rather to "depart and be with Christ" than to be "caught up into the air" with those that are alive and remain at the 'Coming.' So even if Paul did have occasion again and again to defend his Jewish resurrection-doctrine against the Greek disposition to refine it away into a mere doctrine of immortality, his remedy is not a mere falling back into the crudities of Jewish millenarianism. Least of all could he have sympathized with the nationalistic, and even vindictive spirit of Rev. iv.–xxi., with its great battle of Jerusalem helped by Messiah and the angels, against Rome helped by Satan and the Beast. Paul's doctrine of the resurrection of the "body" by "clothing" of the spirit with a "tabernacle" derived "from heaven," his hope of a messianic Kingdom which is the triumph of humanity under a "secondAdam," has its apocalyptic traits. It is a victory over demonic enemies, "spiritual hosts of wickedness in the heavenly places"; but it has the reserve of an educated Pharisee against the cruder forms of Jewish prophecy. It shows the mind of the cosmopolitan Roman citizen and philosophic thinker, not merely that of the Jewish Zealot.

How salutary if Paul himself could have lived to control the divergent elements among his churches, to check the subjective individualism of the Gnostics on the one hand, and the reactionary tendencies of the orthodox on the other. His parting words to his beloved Philippians are sadly appreciative of how needful it was for their sake that he should "abide in the flesh" (Phil. i. 24). Yet there was one thing still more expedient—that he should abide with them in the spirit. And that is just what we find evidenced in the great 'spiritual' Gospel and its accompanying Epistles from Ephesus.

Debate still rages over a mere name, attached by tradition to these writings that themselves bear no name. The titles prefixed by early transcribers attribute them to "John." But they are never employed before 175–180 in a way to even remotely suggest that they were then regarded as written by John, or even as apostolic in any sense. And when we trace the tradition back to its earliest form, in the Epilogue attached to the Gospel (John xxi.) it seems to be no more than a dubious attempt to identify that mysterious figure, the "disciple whom Jesus loved." If, however, we postpone this question raised by the Epilogue, the writings can at least be assigned to a definite locality

(Ephesus) and a fairly definite date (*c.* 105–110), with the general consent both of ancient tradition and of modern criticism. This is for us the important thing, since it enables us to understand their purpose and bearing; whereas even those who contend that they were written by the Apostle John can make little use of the alleged fact. For (1) the little that is known of John from other sources is completely opposed to the characteristics of these writings. They are characterized by a broad universalism, and reproduce the mysticism of Paul. To attribute them to the Pillar of Gal. ii. 9, or the Galilean fisherman of Mark i. 19 and ix. 38, it becomes necessary to suppose that John after migrating to Ephesus underwent a transformation so complete as to make him in reality another man. (2) The meagre possibility that the basis of Revelation might represent the Apostle John becomes more remote than ever. Now it is a curious fact that critics who hold to the much-disputed tradition that the Apostle John wrote the Gospel and Epistles, although these writings make no such claim, and have no affinity with the known character, show as a rule remarkable alacrity to dismiss the claims of Revelation, which positively declares John to have been its author, and has far stronger evidence, both internal and external, in support of the claim, than have either the Gospel or the Epistles. We may prefer the style and doctrine of the Gospel and

Epistles, but this playing fast and loose with the evidence can only discredit criticism of this type. (3) The value of the demonstration of Johannine authorship would lie in the fact that we should then have a first-hand witness to the actual life and teaching of Jesus, immeasurably superior to the remote and indirect tradition of the present Synoptic sources But as a matter of real fact those who maintain the Johannine authorship do not venture to assert any such historical superiority. On the contrary they consider the Synoptic tradition not only historically superior to "John," as respects both sayings and course of events, but they are apt to attribute to this Galilean apostle an extreme of Philonic abstraction, so that he even prefers deliberate "fiction" to fact. Thus the reasoning employed to defend the tradition destroys the only factor which could give it value.

On the other hand it is possible to disregard these secondary disputes, which aim only to increase or diminish the authority of the writings by asserting or denying that they were written by the Apostle John, and to approach the interpretation of them on the basis only of what is really known, accredited both by ancient tradition and by modern criticism. On this basis we can safely affirm that they originated in Ephesus early in the second century, 'spiritualizing' what we have designated 'apostolic' teaching, while at the same time strongly reacting against Doketic and

Antinomian heresy. By such a procedure we shall be employing modern critical methods to the highest practical advantage in the interest of genuinely historical interpretation.

Even those who find minute distinctions in style and point of view between the Epistles and Gospel of John will admit that all four documents emanate from the same period, situation, and circumstances, and represent the same school of thought. We shall make no serious mistake, then, if we treat them as written by the same individual, and even as intended to accompany one another. We shall have the example of so high an authority as Lightfoot, who considered 1st John an Epilogue composed to accompany the Gospel in place of the present Epilogue (John xxi.). Moreover the distinctions in the ancient treatment of 1st John and the two smaller Epistles are all subsequent to the attribution of the Gospel and First Epistle to the Apostle, and a consequence of it. For 1st John and the Gospel had always been inseparable, and having no name attached could easily be treated as the Apostle's. But 2nd and 3rd John distinctly declare themselves written by an "Elder"; and in the days when men still appreciated the distinction between an Elder and an Apostle it was felt to be so serious a difficulty that 2nd and 3rd John were put in the class of "disputed" writings. In reality 1st John and the Gospel are just as certainly the work of an "Elder" as 2nd John and 3rd

John, though no declaration to that effect is made. Moreover 1st John and the Gospel may safely be treated as from the same author; for such minute differences as exist in style and point of view can be fully accounted for by the processes of revision the Gospel has demonstrably undergone. This is more reasonable than to imagine two authors so extraordinarily similar to one another and extraordinarily different from everybody else.

"The Elder" does not give his name, and it is hopeless for us to try to guess it, though it was of course well known to his "beloved" friend "Gaius," to whom the third letter (the outside envelope) was addressed. We have simply three epistles, one (3rd John) personal, to the aforesaid Gaius, who is to serve as the writer's intermediary with "the church," because Diotrephes, its bishop, violently opposes him. Another (2nd John) is addressed to a particular church ("the elect lady and her children"), in all probability the church of Diotrephes and Gaius. It may be the letter referred to in 3rd John 9. The third (1st John) is entirely general, not even so much modified from the type of the homily toward that of the epistle as Hebrews or James; for it has neither superscription nor epistolary close. And yet it is, and speaks of itself (i. 4; ii. 1, 7, 9, 12–14, etc.) as a literary product. It is not impossible that this group of 'epistles,' one individual, one to a particular church, one general, was composed after the plan of the similar group addressed by Paul to churches of this same region, Philemon, Colossians, and the more general epistle known to us as Ephesians. They may have been intended to accompany and introduce the Gospel written by the same author, just as the prophecies of Rev. iv.–xxi. are introduced by the 'epistles' of Rev. i.–iii., or as Luke-Acts is sent under enclosure to Theophilus for publication under his patronage. At all events, be the connection with the Gospel closer or more remote, to learn anything really reliable about the writer and his purpose and environment we must begin with his own references to them, first in the letter to Gaius, then in that to "the elect lady and her children," then in his 'word of exhortation' to young and old, of 1st John. Thus we shall gain a historical approach finally to that treatise on the manifestation of God in Christ which has won him the title since antiquity of the 'theologian.'

Third John shows the author to be a man of eminence in the (larger ?) church whence he writes, old enough to speak of Gaius with commendation as one of his "children," though Gaius himself is certainly no mere youth, and eminent enough to call Diotrephes to answer for his misconduct. He has sent out evangelistic workers, some of whom have recently returned and borne witness "before the church" to their hospitable reception by Gaius. For this he thanks Gaius, and urges him to continue the good work. The main object of the letter, however, is to commend Demetrius, who is doubtless the bearer of this letter as well as another written "to the church" (2nd John ?). This letter, the author fears, will never reach its destination if Diotrephes has his way. There is very little to indicate whence the opposition of Diotrephes arises, but what little there is (ver. 11) points to those who make claims to "seeing" God and being "of" Him, without adequate foundation in a life of purity and beneficence. The letter "to the church" is more explicit.

Second John is perfectly definite in its purpose. After congratulating the "elect lady" on those of her children (members) whom the writer has found leading consistent Christian lives, he entreats the church to remember the "new commandment" of Jesus, which yet is not new but the foundation of all, the commandment of ministering love. The reason for this urgency is that "many deceivers are gone forth into the world, even they that confess not that Jesus Christ cometh in the flesh" (ver. 7). And here we come upon a very novel and distinctive application of an ancient datum of 'prophecy,' clearly differentiating this writer from the author of Revelation. The Doketic heresy is explicitly identified with "the deceiver and the antichrist." That must have been a new and surprising turn for men accustomed to connect the antichrist idea with the persecuting power of Rome. Satan, as we know, had been repeatedly conceived as operating through the coercion of outward force brought against the Messiah and his people through the Beast and the false Prophet (Rev. xiii.). There was good authority, too, for a mystical " man of sin " setting himself forth as God in the temple (2nd Thess. ii. 4), or for connecting Daniel's " abomination that maketh desolate " with the sufferings of the Jewish war and the later attempts of false prophets to deceive the elect with lying wonders (2nd Thess. ii. 9; Mark xiii. 22; Rev. xiii. 14). But this was a new application of the prophecy. To declare that the heretical teachers were themselves antichrists was to call the attention of the church back from outward opposition to inward disloyalty as the greater peril. And the identification is not enunciated in this general warning alone, but fully developed and defended in two elaborate paragraphs of the ' word of exhortation ' (1st John ii. 18–29; iv. 1–6). When, therefore, we find Polycarp in his letter (110–171) quietly adopting the idea, almost as an understood thing, declaring " For every one who shall not confess that Jesus Christ is come in the flesh, is antichrist " (vii. 1), it becomes almost a certainty that he had read 1st John.[1]

[1] Not 2nd John; for it is only in 1st John ii. 18 that the elder speaks of " many antichrists," identifying each separate Doketist with the apocalyptic figure. In 2nd John vii. it is the heresy itself as a phenomenon which constitutes *the* antichrist.

Our elder's warning "to the church" (perhaps more particularly its governing body) is to beware of these deceivers; not to receive them, nor even to greet them, because they "go onward" (are 'progressives') and do not "abide in the teaching of Christ." To abide in this "teaching" is the church's only safeguard.

If next we turn to the more general epistle known as 1st John the lack of any superscription is more than counterbalanced by the writer's full and explicit declarations regarding motive and occasion. The epistle was certainly intended to be read before entire congregations. Of part of it at least the author himself says that it was "written concerning them that would lead you astray" (ii. 26). Comparison of the full denunciation with what we know of Doketism from its own writings, such as the so-called *Acts of John* (*c.* 175), shows very plainly what type of heresy is meant. Moreover we have the Epistles of Ignatius, written to these same churches but a few years later, and the detailed descriptions of the Doketist Cerinthus and his doctrines given by Irenæus, together with the explicit statement that the writings of John were directed against this same Cerinthus.

Yet 1st John is far more than a mere polemic. The author writes to those "that believe on the name of the Son of God, that they may know that they have eternal life" (v. 13) This certainly is the result of the conscious indwelling of the Spirit of Jesus. It is not evidenced, however, by boastful words as to illumination, insight and knowledge, but by practical obedience to the one new commandment; for "God is love, and he that *loveth* (not he that hath *gnosis*) is begotten of God and knoweth God." This inward witness of the Spirit is a gift, or (to use our author's term) an "anointing" (*i. e.* a 'Christ'-ening), whose essence is as much beyond the Greek's ideal of wisdom, on the one side, as it is beyond the Jew's ideal of miraculous powers on the other. It is a spirit of ministering love corresponding to and emanating from the nature of God himself. This is "the teaching of Christ" in which alone it is safe to "abide."

But again as respects the historic tradition of the church our author is not less emphatic. He values the record of an actual, real, and tangible experience of this manifested life of God in man. The "progressives" may repudiate the mere Jesus of "the flesh," in favour of one who comes by water only (*i.e.* in the outpouring of the Spirit in baptism), and not by the blood of the cross. For the doctrine of the cross was a special stumbling-block to Doketists, who rejected the sacrament of the bread and wine.[1] The actual

[1] In the *Acts of John* the Christ spirit which had been resident in Jesus comes to John after he has fled to a cave on the Mount of Olives from the posse that arrested the Lord. The sweet voice of the invisible Christ informs

sending of God's only-begotten Son into the world, the real "propitiation" for our sins (so lightly denied by the illuminati), is a vital point to the writer. The sins "of the whole world" were atoned for in Jesus' blood actually shed on Calvary. The church possesses, then, in this story a record of fact of infinite significance to the world. The Doketists are playing fast and loose with this record of the historic Jesus. They deny any value to the "flesh" in which the æon Christ had merely tabernacled as its "receptacle" between the period of the baptism and the ascension—an event which they date *before* the death on the cross:[1] They are met here with a peremptory challenge and declaration. The experience of contact with the earthly Jesus which the Church cherishes as its most inestimable treasure is the assurance, and the only assurance that we have, of real fellowship with the Father; for "the life, the eternal life" of God in man, the Logos—to borrow frankly the Stoic expression—is known not by mere mystical dreams, but by the historic record of those who personally knew the real Jesus. The manifestation of God, in

---

him there that the blinded multitude below had tortured a mere bodily shape which they took to be Christ, "while I stood by and laughed." In the *Gospel of Peter* Jesus hung upon the cross "as one who feels no pain" and was "taken up" before the end.

[1] See note preceding.

short, is objective and historical, and not merely inward and self-conscious; and that outward and objective manifestation may be summed up in what we of the Christian brotherhood have seen and known of Jesus.

It is when we approach the Fourth Gospel by way of its own author's adaptation of his message to the conditions around him that we begin to appreciate it historically, and in its true worth. The spirit of polemic is still prominent in 1st John, but the Gospel shows the effect of opposition only in the more careful statement of the evangelist's exact meaning. It is a theological treatise, an interpretation of the doctrine of the person of Christ, written that the readers "may believe that Jesus is the Christ, the Son of God, and that believing they may have life in his name" (xx. 31). In an age so eagerly bent on ascertaining the historic facts regarding Jesus' life, and the true sequence of events (Luke i. 1–4), it is insupposable that an author so strenuous to uphold the concrete reality of the church's historic tradition should not give real history so far as he was able. He could not afford to depreciate it in the face of Doketic myth and fancy and contempt for a "Christ in the flesh." The idea that such a writer could deliberately prefer fiction to fact is most improbable; ten times more so if he was the only surviving representative of the twelve, a Galilean disciple even more intimate than Peter with Jesus from the outset. But real history was no longer attainable. The author of the Fourth Gospel reports no event which he does not take in good faith to be fact. Yet it must be apparent from his own statement of his purpose as well as from the very structure of the book that he does not aim to be a historian, but an interpreter of doctrine. He aims to give not *fact* but *truth.* And his handling of (supposed) fact has the freedom we should expect in a church teacher of that age, and of the school of Paul the mystic. The seven progressive " signs " that he narrates, culminating in the raising of Lazarus, are avowedly (xx. 31) illustrative selections from a multitude of current tales of miracle, aiming to produce that faith in Jesus as the Son of God which will result in " life," *i. e.* the eternal life which consists in his indwelling (1st John v. 20). They are not described as acts of pity, drawn from one with whom the power of God was found present to heal. Jesus does not yield as in the Synoptics when compassion for trusting need overcomes reluctance to increase the importunity that interfered with his higher mission. Their prime purpose is to " manifest the glory " of the incarnate Logos, and Jesus performs them only when, and as, he chooses. Pity and natural affection are almost trampled upon that this " manifestation of his glory " may be made more effective (ii. 4; iv. 48; ix. 3; xi. 4–6, 15). As in Paul, there is no exorcism. This most typical and characteristic miracle of Petrine story (Mark iii. 15; Acts x. 38) has disappeared. Or rather (as in Paul) the casting out of Satan from his dominion over the entire world has transcended and superseded it (John xii. 31–33; *cf.* Col. ii. 15). In John, requests for miracle, whether in faith or unbelief, always incur rebuke (ii. 4; iv. 48; vi. 30–36; vii. 4–7; xi. 3–15). Jesus offers and works them when "his hour" comes, whether applied for or not (v. 6–9; vi. 6; ix. 1–7). His reserve is not due to a limitation of almighty power; for the power is declared explicitly to be his, *in his own right* (v. 21; xi. 22, 25, 42). He restrains it only that faith may rest upon conviction of the truth rather than mere wonder (ii. 23–25; iii. 2 *f.*; iv. 39–42, 48; vi. 29–46; xiv. 11). He is, in short, an omniscient (i. 47–50; ii. 25), omnipotent Being, temporarily sojourning on the earth (iii. 13; xvi. 28).

The dialogue interwoven with these seven signs is closely related in subject to them. It does not aim to repeat remembered Sayings, but follows that literary form which since Plato had been the classic model for presenting the themes of philosophy. The subject-matter is no longer, as in the Synoptics, the Righteousness required by God, the Nature and Coming of the Kingdom, Duty to God and Man. It is the person and function of the speaker himself. Instead of the parables we have allegories: "seven 'I am's'" of Jesus, in debate with "the Jews" about the doctrine of his own person as Son of God.

This uniformity of topic corresponds with a complete absence of any attempt to differentiate in style between utterances of Jesus, or the Baptist, or the evangelist himself, in Gospel or Epistles. Had the writer desired, it is certain that he could have collected sayings of Jesus, and given them a form similar to those of Matthew and Luke. He does not try. The only device he employs to suggest a distinction is an oracular ambiguity at first misunderstood, and so requiring progressive unfolding. The main theme is often introduced by a peculiar and solemn "Verily, verily."

As with the 'signs' the lingering Synoptic sense of progress and proportion has disappeared. At the very outset John the Baptist proclaims to his followers that his own baptism has no value in itself. It is not "for repentance unto remission of sins." It is *only* to make the Christ "manifest" (i. 19–34). Christ's atonement alone will take away the sin (i. 29), Christ's baptism alone will convey real help (i. 34). Jesus, too, proclaims himself from the outset the Christ, in the full Pauline sense of the word (i. 45–51; iv. 26, etc.). He chooses Judas with the express purpose of the betrayal, and forces on the reluctant agents of his fate (vi. 70 *f.*; xiii. 26 *f.*; xviii. 4–8; xix. 8–11).

All this, and much more which we need not cite, makes hardly the pretence of being history. It is frankly theology, or rather apologetics. We have as a framework the general outline of Mark, a Galilean and a Judæan ministry (chh. i.–xii.; xiii.–xx.), with traces of a Perean journey (vii. 1 *ff.*). This scheme, however, is broken through by another based on the Mosaic festal system, Jesus showing in each case as he visits Jerusalem, the higher symbolism of the ceremonial (ii. 13 *ff.* Passover; v. 1 *ff.* Pentecost; vii. 1 *ff.* Tabernacles; x. 22 *ff.* Dedication; xii. 1 *ff.* Passover). There is in chh. i.–iv. a 'teaching of baptisms' and of endowment with the Spirit corresponding roughly to Mark i. 1–45. There is in ch. v. a teaching of the authority of Jesus against Moses and the Law, corresponding to Mark ii. 1—iii. 6. There is a teaching of the 'breaking of bread' corresponding to Mark vi. 30—viii. 26 in John vi., though this last has been related not merely to the brotherhood banquet ('love-feast') as in Mark, but anticipates and takes the place of the teaching as to the Eucharist (*cf.* John vi. 52–59 with John xiii.). There is a Commission of the Twelve like Matt. x. 16–42, though placed (with Luke xxii. 35–38) as a second sending on the night of betrayal (xiii. 31—xviii. 26). There is dependence on Petrine Story, and to some extent on Matthæan Sayings. In particular John xii. 1–7 combines the data of Mark xiv. 3–9 with those of Luke vii. 36–50; x. 38–42 in a curious compound, making it certain that the evangelist employed these two—and Matthew as well, if xii. 8 be genuine (it is not found in the ancient Syriac). Yet our Synoptic Gospels are not the only sources, and the material borrowed is handled with sovereign superiority. In short, as even the church fathers recognized, this Gospel is of a new type. It does aim to "supplement" the others, as they recognized; but not as one narrative may piece out and complete another. Rather as the unseen and spiritual supplements the external and visible. This Gospel uses the established forms of miracle-story and saying; but it transforms the one into symbol, the other into dialogue and allegory. Then by use of this material (supplemented from unknown, perhaps oral, sources) it constructs a series of interpretations of the person and work of the God-man.

Of one peculiarly distinctive feature we have still to speak. Where the reader has special need of an interpreter to attest and interpret a specially vital fact, such as the scenes of the night of the betrayal, or the reality of Jesus' propitiatory death (denied by the Doketists), or the beginning of the resurrection faith, Peter's testimony is supplemented and transcended by that of a hitherto unknown figure, who anticipates all that Peter only slowly attains. This is the mysterious, unnamed "disciple whom Jesus loved" (xiii. 23 *ff*.; xviii. 15 *f*.; xix. 25–37; xx. 1–10; *cf*. Gal. xx. 20), a Paul present in the spirit, to see things with the eye of spiritual insight. There is no transfiguration-scene and no prayer of Gethsemane in this Gospel—Transfiguration is needless where the glory shines uninterrupted through the whole career. Prayer itself is impossible where oneness with the God-head makes difference of thought or purpose inconceivable. Hence the prayers of Jesus are often only "for the sake of those that stand by" (xi. 41 *f.*). The same is true of the Voice from heaven at the scene which takes the place of Transfiguration and Gethsemane in one (xii. 27–33). Jesus will not ask for deliverance from that hour, because he had sought it from the beginning. His prayer is "Father, glorify thy name." The Voice, which some take to be an angel speaking to him (*cf.* Luke ix. 35; xxii. 43) is for the sake of the bystanders. The Voice at his baptism likewise is not addressed to him (the incarnate Logos does not need a revelation of his own identity) but to the Baptist.

So again and again Synoptic scenes are retouched and new scenes are added in a way to present a consistent picture of the "tabernacling" of the pre-existent Son of God in human flesh. As we review the whole, and ask ourselves, What is the occasion of this strange new presentation of the evangelic message? we begin to realize how indispensable is the key which the evangelist has himself hung before the door. Many and complex are the problems which confront us as we move through this heaped-up tangle of anecdote, dialogue, and allegory There is room for the keenest scrutiny of criticism to determine, if possible, when, and how, and from what sources these meditations were put together. But nothing that critical insight, analysis, and comparison can furnish avails so much to throw real light upon the work as what the evangelist himself has done, by setting forth in a prologue (i. 1–18) the fundamental principles of his conception.

In a word evangelic tradition as it had hitherto found currency still lacked the fundamental thing in the Christology of Paul—the Incarnation doctrine. Paul conceived the story of Jesus as a supernal drama, beginning and ending in heaven at God's right hand. Even Matthew and Luke, carrying back the adoption to Sonship from the baptism to the birth of Jesus, had not essentially changed the pre-Pauline point of view. Still there was no pre-existence. Jesus was not yet shown as the Wisdom of God, through whom all things were created, the " heavenly man," the second Adam, taking upon him the form of a servant, humbling himself and becoming obedient unto death, rich, and for our sakes becoming poor. He was still, even in Mark, just the prophet mighty in deed and word, raised up by God from among his brethren, and for his obedience exalted to the messianic throne of glory. How *could* this satisfy churches trained in the doctrine of Paul ? We should almost rather marvel that the Synoptic narratives ever found lodgment at all, where Paul had preached from the beginning a doctrine of the eternal Christ.

And the transformation is not one whit more radical than we ought to anticipate. The Transfiguration story had been a halting attempt to embody Pauline doctrine in Petrine story. But apart from the obvious hold afforded to mere Doketism, how inadequate to Paul's conception of the "Man from heaven"! The Fourth evangelist depicts the person of Jesus consistently and throughout, despite his meagre and refractory material, along the lines of Pauline Christology. There is no concession to Doketism, for in spite of all, and designedly (iv. 6; xix. 28, 34), Jesus is still no phantasm, but true man among men. There is no hesitation to override, where needful, on vital points the great and growing authority of 'apostolic' tradition. Tacitly, but uncompromisingly, Petrine tradition is set aside. The "disciple whom Jesus loved" sees the matter otherwise. In particular, apocalyptic eschatology is firmly repressed in favour of a doctrine of eternal life in the Spirit. The second Coming is not to be a manifestation "to the world." It will be an inward indwelling of God and Christ in the heart of the believer (xiv. 22 *f.*).[1] The place of future reward is

[1] Some few passages inconsistent with this are found in the body of the Gospel. Like that of the appendix (xxi. 22) they are later modifications of a doctrine too Hellenic for the majority.

not a glorified Palestine and transfigured, rebuilt Jerusalem. The disciple, like Paul, will " depart to be with Christ." The Father's house is wider than the Holy Land. It has " many mansions," and the servant must be content to know that his Master will receive him where he dwells himself (xiv. 1–3; xvii. 24).

To realize what it meant to produce the 'spiritual' Gospel that comes to us from Ephesus shortly after the close of the first century we must place ourselves side by side with men who had learned the gospel of Paul *about* Jesus, the drama of the eternal, pre-existent, " heavenly Man," incarnate, triumphant through the cross over the Prince of this world and powers of darkness. We must realize how they found it needful to impregnate the 'apostolic' material of Petrine and Matthæan tradition with this deeper significance, preserving the concrete, historic fact, and the real manhood, and yet supplementing the disproportionately external story with a wealth of transcendental meaning. The spirit of Paul was, indeed, not dead. Neither Gnostic heresy could dissipate it, nor reactionary Christianized legalism absorb it. It had been reborn in splendid authority and power. In due time it would prove itself the very mould of 'catholic' doctrine. The Fourth gospel, as its Prologue forewarns, is an application to the story of Jesus as tradition reported it of the Pauline incarnation doctrine formulated under the Stoic Logos theory. It represents a study in the psychology of religion applied to the person of Christ. Poor as Paul himself in knowledge of the outward Jesus, unfamiliar with really historical words and deeds, its doctrine *about* Jesus became, nevertheless, like that of the great Apostle to the Gentiles, the truest exposition of 'the heart of Christ.'

CHAPTER X

EPILOGUES AND CONCLUSIONS

FEW of the great writings cherished and transmitted by the early church have escaped the natural tendency to attachments at beginning and end. In the later period such attachments took the form of prefixed *argumenta, i. e.* prefatory descriptions of author and contents, and affixed *subscriptions*, devoted to a similar purpose. These, like the titles, were clearly distinguished from the text itself, and in modern editions are usually not printed, though examples of 'subscriptions' may be seen in the King James version after the Pauline Epistles. Before the time when canonization had made such a process seem sacrilege they were attached to the text itself, with greater or less attempt to weld the parts together. We need not add to what has been already said as to certain superscriptions of the later epistolary literature, such as James and Jude, where the relation to the text impresses us as closer than is sometimes admitted; nor need we delay with the preamble to Revelation (Rev. i. 1–3). That which has been added at the close, in cases where real evidence exists of such later supplementation, is of special significance to our study, inasmuch as it tends to throw light where light is most required. For that is an obscure period, early in the second century, when not only the churches themselves were drawing together toward catholic unity under the double pressure of inward and outward peril, but were bringing with them their treasured writings, sometimes a collection of Epistles, sometimes a Gospel, or a book of Prophecy, sometimes, as in the groups of writings attributed to John and Peter, a full canon of Gospel, Epistles and Apocalypse, followed but little later by 'Acts' as well.

The most ancient list of books authorized to be publicly read that we possess is that of the church of Rome *c.* 185, called after its discoverer the Canon of Muratori. From this fragment, mutilated at beginning and end, we learn that Paul's letters to the churches were arranged in a group of seven[1] of which Romans stood last. It is probably due to its position at the end that Romans has been supplemented by the addition of Pauline fragments, which did not appear in some early editions of the text. The letter proper ends with ch. xv. though xvi. 21–23 probably

[1] The personal letters formed a separate group. Two letters to the same church (1st Cor., 2nd Cor.) were counted as one. Marcion (140) counted ten in all, and had a different order.

followed, perhaps concluding with ver. 24, which some texts insert after ver. 19. Ver. 25–27 is another fragment omitted in some texts.

We have seen above (p. 200) how Revelation has received conclusion after conclusion, so that the relation of personalities has become almost unintelligible. We have very meagre textual material for Revelation, and can scarcely judge whether any of the process represented in Rev. xxii. 6–21 belongs to the period of transmission, after the publication of the book in its present form. Until the discovery of new textual evidence the phenomena in Revelation must be treated by principles of the higher criticism, as pertaining to its history before publication. At all events we know that the attribution to "John" (ver. 8 *f*.) was current as early as Justin's *Apology* (153).

The longer and shorter supplements to Mark belong again to the field of textual criticism. The manuscripts and early translations carry us back to a time when neither ending was known; though only to leave us wondering how the necessity arose for composing them—a question of the higher criticism. Mark xvi. 9–20 shows acquaintance with Luke, and probably with John xx. It is noteworthy, however, in view of the author's attempt to cover the resurrection appearances of these two gospels, that he betrays no sign of acquaintance with John xxi. In this case of the Roman gospel, however, textual evidence enables us to trace something of the history of supplementation. The so-called 'Shorter' ending provides a close for the incomplete story, resembling Matthew, while the 'Longer' is drawn from Luke and John. i.–xx. Subsequent employments show that the 'Longer' ending had been attached (perhaps at Rome) not later than *c.* 150. It is the first evidence we have of combination of the Fourth gospel with the Synoptics; for even Justin, though *affected* by John, does not *use* it as he uses Matthew, Mark and Luke. Parity among the four is not traceable earlier than Tatian (*c.* 175), the father of gospel 'harmonies.' The 'Shorter' ending, if not the Longer as well, would seem to have been added in Egypt. The supplements to Mark have this at least of singular interest, that they show the progress of a process whose beginnings we traced back to Palestine itself in the church of the 'apostles, elders and witnesses of the Lord,' where "the Elder" in the tradition reported by Papias is already offering explanations of the disagreements of Matthew and Mark with a view to their concurrent circulation.

After the addition of Mark to Matthew it was comparatively easy to take in Luke–Acts as a third, and to form composites out of the three such as the *Gospel of Peter* (North Syria *c.* 130) and the *Gospel of the Nazarenes* (Coele-Syria *c.* 140). Justin at Rome (*c.* 153) is still such a three-gospel man, though affected by the Fourth; whereas his predecessor Hermas (125–140) seems to rest on Mark alone, though perhaps acquainted with Matthew. The step was a harder one which aimed to take in the Fourth gospel. Tatian at Rome (*c.* 175) and Theophilus at Antioch (181) are the agents of its accomplishment; and, as we have seen, it was not effected without a determined opposition, led at Rome by the presbyter Gaius, and answered by Irenæus (*c.* 186) and Hippolytus (*c.* 215). Such opposition from the side of advocates of Petrine apostolicity is anticipated in the most significant and important of all the epilogues, the so-called Appendix or Epilogue to the Fourth gospel (John xxi.).

Just when, or where, this supplement was added is one of the most difficult problems of the higher criticism. On the side of external evidence we have the fact that it shows no effect in Mark xvi. 9–21, where John xx is employed, and that there is a great change about A.D. 170 in the treatment of this Gospel and its related Epistles, those who use them before this time showing no disposition to treat them as having high apostolic authority. On the side of internal evidence there are such data as the use of the second-century name for the Sea of Galilee ("Sea of Tiberias," xxi. 1), and references to the martyrdom of Peter at Rome (xxi. 18 *f.*) and to legends of John as the 'witness' who should survive until the Coming (xxi. 23). Whether these data suggest an origin at Ephesus, or at Rome, and at just what date, are problems for technical research. That which is of chief interest for us is the motive and function of this supplement to the Ephesian Gospel, and the light it throws upon conditions in the church at large.

It is quite apparent that John xxi. forms a subsequent attachment after the formal conclusion of the Gospel proper in xx. 30 *f*. For, apart from differences in style and doctrinal standpoint, it makes a complete new departure along the lines of Mark's story of Galilean resurrection manifestations; whereas the Gospel follows the Lukan type, and brings everything to a close without removal from Jerusalem. The message to the disciples by the women at the sepulchre is here given by Jesus in person as in Matt. xxviii. 10, and is actually delivered as in Luke xxiv. 10 *f*. It is followed by the promised manifestation to the disciples with the overcoming of their incredulity, and by the great Commission, accompanied by the Gift of the Spirit. The story has thus been brought to a formal conclusion, the invariable and necessary conclusion of all evangelic narratives. The author's recapitulation of the nature and contents of his book and assurance in direct address to the reader of his purpose in writing ("that *ye* may believe") follows appropriately as a winding up of the whole. It is not conceivable that the same writer should resume immediately after this, at an earlier point in the narrative, where the disciples are still scattered in Galilee, unconscious of their vocation and commission. For in spite of the endeavour of the supplementer in ver. 14 to make this out " the third[1] time that Jesus was manifested " they have manifestly returned to their original means of livelihood unawakened to the resurrection faith. Moreover the story culminates with a restoration of Peter to favour, with unmistakable reference to his humiliating failure to live up to the promise (xiii. 36–38), " Lord, why cannot I follow thee even now ? I will lay down my life for thee " (*cf.* xxi. 15–19). If it had been the evangelist's intention to tell this he would have told it before the Commission in xx. 19–23. In short, we have here two widely variant forms of the tradition of the rallying of the disciples from their unbelief by the risen Christ and commissioning of them to their task. The two commissions, one a general commission of all " the twelve," like Matt. xviii. 18, the other a special commission of Peter like Matt. xvi. 19, are attached one after the other, with the curious infelicity that the restoration of Peter from his defection, together with his installation as chief under-shepherd of the flock, comes *after* the commission in which

[1] A miscount for "fourth," unless we disregard xx. 11–18, or else (with Wellhausen) consider xx. 24–29 an insertion later than the Epilogue.

he has already appeared with the rest, restored to full faith and favour, and gifted with the inspiration and authority of the Spirit.

It is true that the function of "tending the flock of God" (*cf.* 1st Pet. v. 2) committed to Peter in xxi. 15–19 is a more special one than the apostolate conferred on all in xx. 21–23; but the Epilogue has previously (xxi. 1–14) given to Peter a special and commanding part in the apostolate (extension of the gospel to the world). No one will question that in such a writer as the Fourth evangelist (and if anything still more the writer of the Epilogue) narratives of miracle are intended to have a symbolical sense. Nor will it be denied that the miraculous draft of fishes, which in Luke v. 1–11 attends the original vocation of "Simon,"[1] is here applied to the work the twelve are to accomplish in the now opening future as "fishers of men." The particularization of the number of the fishes, and the statement that the peril of the rending of the net (*cf.* Luke v. 6) was happily avoided, are, of course, also intended to convey a symbolical sense, which Jerome makes still easier to grasp by informing us that 153 was taken by naturalists of the time to be the full number of all species of fish. John xxi. 1–14 is therefore a primitive story of the

[1] The addition in ver. 10*a* and the plural "they" in ver. 11, are mere editorial adaptations of the story to Mark i. 16–20.

appearance of Jesus after his resurrection "to Peter and them that were with him," in Galilee (not in Jerusalem as in John i.–xx. and Luke), having a relation to Luke v. 1–11, and probably also to Matt. xiv. 28–33 (*cf.* John xxi. 7). It is also nearly akin to the fragment at the end of the *Gospel of Peter*. It symbolizes the work of the apostolic mission under the figure of the fishing of men (*cf.* Mark i. 17; Matt. xiii. 47–50), and gives to Peter the leading part. In fact Peter not only comes to the Lord in advance of all the rest, and alone maintains with him something like the intimate relations of the past, but performs after his private interview with Jesus the gigantic feat of bringing unaided to land the entire miraculous catch. The great and various multitude, which all working in common had enclosed in the net, but had not been able to lift into the boat, Peter, at Jesus' word, brought safely home. The writer who so employs the already conventionalized symbols of ecclesiastical imagery, surely had no mean idea of the apostleship of Peter. In at least as high degree as the author of Acts he conceives of Peter as commissioned in a special sense to be the great director and leader of all missionary activity, to Gentiles as well as Jews (Acts xv. 7), and to have been the saviour of the unity of the church in the hour of its threatened disruption. When in addition he is invested by Jesus with the insignia and office of chief under-shepherd of the flock of God, the stain of his threefold denial wiped out by a threefold opportunity to prove his special love by special service, and the ignominy of his previous failure to "follow" (xiii. 36–38) atoned for by the promise that in old age he shall have opportunity to follow Jesus in martyrdom (xxi. 18 *f.*), there remains nothing that the most exacting friend of 'catholic' apostolicity could demand in the way of tribute to its great representative.

And yet the main object of the Epilogue has not yet been touched. It was not written, we may be sure, merely to glorify Peter; though it is, of course, insupposable that the Gospel in its primitive form simply left Peter in the attitude of a renegade after xviii. 27, to reappear quite as if nothing had happened in xx. 1 *ff.*[1] It pays its tribute to Peter as chief witness to the resurrection, chief apostle, chief saviour of the unity of the church, chief under-shepherd of the flock of God, in the interest of that catholic apostolic unity which all churchmen were so earnestly labouring to achieve in the writer's time, and for which the name of Peter was increasingly significant. But the chief object of the Epilogue is something else. It was written primarily to commend and find room

[1] We must conclude that *both* these data from Synoptic tradition, the denial (xiii. 36–38; xviii. 15–18, 25–27) *and* the restoration (ch. xxi.) are supplements to the original form of the Gospel.

for another authority, the authority of the Gospel to which it is appended, and which repeatedly sets over against Peter a mysterious unnamed figure, who always sees when Peter is blind, believes when Peter is unbelieving, is faithful when Peter and all the rest have fled in cowardly desertion. The object of the Epilogue is to find room alongside the growing and salutary authority of Peter for the authority and message of "the disciple whom Jesus loved." Its purpose appears in its conclusion, "This (the disciple whom Jesus loved) is the disciple which beareth witness of these things, and wrote these things, and we (the church which cherishes and gives forth this 'spiritual' Gospel) know that his witness is true."

The writer does not explicitly say that he means the Apostle John (reputed in Ephesus the author of Revelation); for such direct identification might well endanger his own object. But he makes it clear in two ways that John is really intended, as, indeed, subsequent writers immediately infer.[1] (1) "The sons of Zebedee" are introduced for the first time in the entire work in xxi. 2, among the group who are present with Peter. An easy process of elimination,[2] then, leaves

[1] The *Muratorianum* bases its legendary account of the writing of the Fourth gospel by "John" with the endorsement of "his fellow-disciples and bishops" on John xxi. 24.

[2] The early death of James the son of Zebedee (Acts xii. 1) excludes him from consideration.

open to identification as "the disciple whom Jesus loved" (ver. 7) only John, or else one of the two unnamed "other disciples," who could hardly be reckoned among Jesus' closest intimates.

(2) The scene of the prediction of Peter's martyrdom (xxi. 18 *f.*) is followed immediately (ver. 20–23) by a reference to traditions which we know to have been current before the close of the first century regarding the martyrdom of the two sons of Zebedee, in particular regarding John. Peter in xxi. 21 raises the question as to the *fate* of "the disciple whom Jesus loved" (literally, "and as to this man, what?"). The pregnant command of Jesus to Peter, "Follow me," is clearly intended to have reference to martyrdom (*cf.* xiii. 36 *f.*), and it is obeyed by "the disciple whom Jesus loved" as well as Peter. Peter's inquiry and the Lord's reply had given rise "among the brethren" to the belief that this disciple would "tarry" till the Coming. Now it is of John, son of Zebedee, and only of him, that we have a curious vacillation of ancient tradition between belief in his martyrdom in the same sense as his brother James (Mark x. 39), and a belief (probably based on Mark ix. 1) that he would tarry as an abiding witness until the Coming ('white martyrdom'). The writer of the Epilogue has manifestly these traditions about the fate of John in mind. He would have his readers understand that the enigmatic

prophecy of Jesus neither promised the permanent survival of John, nor his violent death, but was at least capable of an interpretation which set John alongside of Peter, not as a rival of his leadership, or directive control, but simply as a witness ('martyr') to the truth. Peter is willingly granted the office of 'ruling elder' in the church, if only "the disciple whom Jesus loved" may have the function of the prophet and teacher 'in the Spirit,' the man of faith and insight, whose function it is to interpret 'the mind of Christ.'

Few things could be more significant of the conditions of Christian life and thought in the earlier years of the second century than this Epilogue, appended to the 'spiritual' Gospel to commend it to general acceptance in the church. It is not vitally important whether the cautiously suggested identification of the Beloved Disciple with John, the son of Zebedee, be correct or not. It is important to a historical appreciation of the great literary contribution of the churches of Paul to the 'catholic' Christianity of the second century, that we realize what Petrine catholicity had then come to mean, and how the Pauline spiritual gospel came half-way to meet it. On this point a study of the epilogues is rewarding, but especially of the great Epilogue to the Gospel of John.

We have reached the period for our own

concluding words. The process of combination and canonization of the New Testament writings, which followed upon the consolidation of the churches in the second century falls outside our province. We have sought only to give some insight into the origins, considering the Making of the New Testament to apply rather to the creations of the formative period, when conscious inspiration was still in its full glow, than to the period of collection into an official canon. As we look back over the two leading types of Christian thought, Pauline and 'Apostolic,' the Greek-Christian gospel *about* Jesus, and the Jewish-Christian gospel *of* Jesus, the gospel of the Spirit and the gospel of authority, we cannot fail to realize how deep and broad and ancient are the two great currents of religious thought and life that here are mingling, contending, coming to new expression and clearer definition. Each has its various subdivisions and modifications, Pauline Christianity in the Greek world has its problems of resistance to Hellenistic perversion on the one side, to reaction toward Jewish external authority on the other. Apostolic Christianity whether in its more conservative form at Jerusalem, or in broader assimilation to Pauline doctrine at Antioch and Rome, has also its divergent streams, its more primitive and its more developed stages. The literature, as we slowly come to appreciate it against the background of the times, more and more reveals itself as an index to the life. Not to the mere idiosyncrasies of individuals, but to the great Gulf-stream of the human instinct for social Righteousness and for individual Redemption, as it sweeps onward in its mighty tide.

The literature of the New Testament must be understood historically if understood at all. It must be understood as the product, we might almost say the precipitate, of the greatest period in the history of religion. It represents the meeting and mutual adjustment of two fundamental and complementary conceptions of religion. The antithesis is not merely that between the particularism of the Jew and the universalism of the Gentile. It is an antithesis of the social ideal of Law and Prophets against the individual ideal of personal redemption through union with the divine Spirit, which lay at the heart of all vital Hellenistic religious thought in this period of the Empire. Christianity as we know it, the religion of humanity as it has come to be, the ultimate world-religion as we believe it destined to become, is a resultant of these two factors, Semitic and Aryan, the social and the individual ideal. Its canonized literature represents the combination. On the one side the social ideal is predominant. It perpetuates the gospel *of* Jesus in the form of Matthæan and Petrine tradition, supplemented by apocalypse, which tradition attaches conjecturally to the name of John.

The goal it seeks is the Kingdom of God, righteousness and peace on earth as in heaven. On the other side the individual ideal predominates. It perpetuates the gospel *about* Jesus in the form of the Pauline and Johannine doctrine of his person, regarded as the norm and type of spiritual life. The goal it seeks is personal immortality by moral fellowship with God. Its faith is Sonship, by participation in the divine nature, without limitation in time, without loss of individual identity. Both types of gospel are justified in claiming to emanate from Jesus of Nazareth; but neither without the other can claim to fully represent the significance of his spirit and life.

The unity of the New Testament is a unity in diversity. Just because it presents so widely divergent conceptions of what the gospel is, it gives promise of perennial fecundity. Studied not after the manner of the scribes, who think that in their book of precept and prophecy they have a passport to rewards in a magical world to come, but studied as a " manifestation of the life, even the eternal life " of the Spirit of God in man, it will continue to reproduce the spirit and mind of Christ. Studied as a reflection at various times and in divers manners of that redemptive Wisdom of God, which " in every generation entering into holy souls makes men to be prophets and friends of God " (Sap. vii. 27), and which the Greeks, considering it, unfortunately, in its intellectual rather than its moral aspect, call the Logos of God, it will prove, as in so many generations past it has proved, an "incorruptible seed," a "word of good tidings preached unto" the world, a "word of the Lord that abideth for ever."

BIBLIOGRAPHY

1. General Introductions to N.T. Literature.

MOFFATT, JAS. "*Internat. Theol. Library*" *Series*. Scribner's, 1911. Standard, comprehensive, progressive. Best compendium of the subject in English. A book for experts. 671 pp., 8vo.

JÜLICHER, A. Engl. transl., by D. A. Ward, from 4th German ed. London, Smith, Elder & Co., 1903. The most serviceable of modern German Introductions, based on the standard work of the "liberal" school, by H. J. Holtzmann. 650 pp., large 8vo.

ZAHN, THEO. Engl. transl. from 3rd German ed., by M. W. Jacobus. Scribner's, 1909. Standard "conservative" work. Immense scholarship in the harness of apologetics. Total, 1750 pp., in 3 vols., large 8vo.

BACON, B. W. "*New Test. Handbook*" *Series*. Macmillan 1900. Similar to Moffatt's in standpoint, but without the survey of the literature. For readers less technically advanced. 300 pp., small 8vo.

PEAKE, A. S. N.Y., Scribner's, 1910. 250 pp., 12mo. An excellent primer of the subject, generally conservative.

2. Critical Treatments of Pauline Literature.

SHAW, R. D. *The Pauline Epistles, Introductory and Expository Studies*, 2nd ed. T. & T. Clarke, 1904. 518 pp., large 8vo. Sober and cautious. For general readers.

RAMSAY, W. M. *Pauline and other Studies in Early Christian History*. Hodder & Stoughton, 1906. 425 pp., large 8vo. *The Cities of St. Paul* (1907, 468 pp.) is by the same author, an eminent geographer and archaeologist ardently enlisted against German criticism. Interesting but diffuse.

PFLEIDERER, O. *Paulinism.* Engl. transl. by E. Peters. 2nd ed. 1891. Williams & Norgate. 2 vols. 8vo. Total, 580 pp., 8vo. Still a standard exposition of Paul's system of thought. A book for experts.

BAUR, F. C. *Paul the Apostle of Jesus Christ, his Life and Work, Epistles and Doctrine.* Engl. transl. of Zeller's (2nd), German ed., by A. Menzies. Williams & Norgate, 1876. Two vols. 8vo (375 + 350 pp.). An epoch-making book, the starting-point of modern criticism.

SCHWEITZER, A. This able, though one-sided, critic has issued already (1912) the conclusion to his study of modern Lives of Christ (see below, *The Quest of the Historical Jesus*) under the title *Geschichte der Paulinischen Forschung.* It may be expected that this comprehensive survey and searching criticism of the literature of Pauline study will soon be made accessible to the English reader.

WREDE, W. *Paul.* Engl. transl. by E. Lummis. P. Green, London, 1907. 190 pp., 12mo. A brief, brilliant, popular sketch, radical, suggestive. Needs the balance of more cautious criticism.

WEISS, J. *Paul and Jesus.* Engl. transl. by H. J. Chaytor. London and New York, Harper & Bros., 1909. 130 pp., 12mo. An effective answer to Wrede's view of Paul as the real creator of Christianity, by a progressive and able critic.

Lives of Paul by Cone, Clemen (German) and others are abundant in recent years. See the *Encyclopaedias* and *Dictionaries of the Bible,* s.v. "Paul."

3. Critical Treatments of the Synoptic Gospels and Acts.

STANTON, V. H. *The Gospels as Historical Documents,* Parts I and II. Cambridge University Press, 1903–1909. 297 + 400 pp., 8vo. A standard survey of Gospel criticism from a conservative standpoint, the work of a scholar for scholars.

CONE, O. *Gospel Criticism and Historical Christianity.* Putnam's, N.Y., 1891. 375 pp., small 8vo. Liberal, semi-popular.

BURKITT, F. C. *The Earliest Sources for the Life of Jesus.* Houghton & Mifflin, Boston and New York, 1910. 130 pp., 12mo. Simple and popular. Burkitt is a leading progressive scholar.

4. The Johannine Writings.

DRUMMOND, JAS. *Character and Authorship of the Fourth Gospel.* Scribner's, N.Y., 1904. 544 pp., 8vo. The ablest recent defence of the traditional authorship. Scholarly discussion of the literary history.

BACON, B. W. *The Fourth Gospel in Research and Debate.* Moffat, Yard & Co., N.Y., 1910. 556 pp., 8vo. A similar discussion of the evidences reaching the reverse conclusion.

SCOTT, E. F. *The Fourth Gospel, its Purpose and Theology.* T. & T. Clarke, Edinburgh, 1906. 386 pp., 8vo. Admirable in temper, lucid in style, semi-popular.

SCHMIEDEL, P. W. *The Johannine Writings.* Engl. transl., by M. A. Canney. London, A. & C. Black, 1903. 295 pp., 12mo. Brief, popular, radical, by one of the ablest of N.T. critics.

General.

REUSS, E. *History of the N.T.* Engl. transl. from 5th German ed., by E. L. Houghton. Boston, Houghton, Mifflin & Co., 1884. 649 pp. 2 vols. large 8vo. A standard treasury of scholarly information.

WERNLE, P. *The Beginnings of Christianity.* Engl. transl., by G. A. Bienemann. London, Williams & Norgate, 1904. 388 + 404 pp., 8vo. 2 vols. Able, scholarly, advanced.

PFLEIDERER, O. *Christian Origins.* Engl. transl., by D. Huebsch. New York, B. W. Huebsch, 1906. 295 pp., 12mo. Popular lectures showing something of the views of the modern school of critics known as *religionsgeschichtlich.* Pfleiderer's critical opinions are fully expressed in his *Primitive Christianity* (Engl. transl., by W. Montgomery, in four vols., 8vo. Putnams, 1909).

MUZZEY, D. S. *The Rise of the N.T.* New York, Macmillan, 1900. 156 pp., 12mo. An excellent primer for beginners.

WREDE, W. *The Origin of the N.T.* Engl. transl. by J. S. Hill. Harper & Bros., London & New York, 1909. 151 pp., 12mo. An admirable primer by a brilliant leader of advanced criticism.

VON SODEN. *The History of Early Christian Literature. Writings of the N.T.* Engl. transl., by J. R. Wilkinson.

Williams & Norgate, 1906. 476 pp., 12mo. A book for beginners by a great N.T. scholar of liberal views. A closely connected field is covered by various *Histories of the Apostolic Age*, of which the most recent and important are those of Weizsäcker (Engl. transl., 1895) and McGiffert (1897). Less technical and more orthodox are those of Vernon-Bartlett (1899) and J. H. Ropes (1906). *Critical Lives of Christ* present the results of critical study of the Gospels. A survey of this field of research, keenly analytical and severely critical, is given by A. Schweitzer in *The Quest of the Historical Jesus* (Engl. transl. by W. Montgomery. A. & C. Black, 1910. 416 pp., 8vo). Schweitzer writes with great scholarship and power, but decided polemic interest as a "consistent eschatologist."

INDEX

Richard Clay & Sons, Limited, London and Bungay.